I0729450

Graciela Iturbide

on Dreams, Symbols, and Imagination

Introduction
by Alfonso Morales Carrillo

Edited by
Alfonso Morales Carrillo
and Mauricio Maillé

aperture

Table of Contents

Introduction

By Alfonso Morales Carrillo

The book you are holding in your hands began in Mexico City, where Graciela Iturbide lives and works, just as everyone in the world was urged to stay home in response to the global pandemic. Mexico City—famous for its gregarious spirit, fueled by its lively people and their capacity to live life on the brink of chaos—became almost unrecognizable without the animated presence of passersby, without their bustle and noise in the streets and plazas. With this as our backdrop, Mauricio Maillé and I worked with Iturbide to form and shape the contents of this book—a new survey of her photographic work, led by her words and thinking, to become part of Aperture's Photography Workshop Series. The world was very different from that of 2018 and 2019 when Maillé and I travelled with Iturbide as she finished her *White Fence* series in Los Angeles, where we witnessed firsthand her close relationships within the Mexican American community she had been photographing since the 1980s. In striking contrast, we had no choice but to make do, at times, with virtual conversations and their illusion of being together in the same space.

Since photography for Iturbide has been a means of discovering her own personal vision, this meant that we got to listen to her most evocative stories and reflections as part of the process. It was a privilege to experience this journey into the corners of her memory and the substrata of her archives. We had no sense of how long the siege of the world-wide pandemic would continue, but working with Iturbide encouraged us through difficult times, and reaffirmed for us photography's capacity to celebrate life in all its variations and dimensions.

We, as editors, recognized the value of her recollections beyond the pleasure of hearing them and beyond their historical interest. By describing the contexts and circumstances in which her photographs were made, Iturbide gave us an opportunity to observe her at work and to accompany her to the places and moments that attracted her attention, or rather awakened her astonishment.

Much like her mentor Manuel Álvarez Bravo, Iturbide does not impose her own way of doing things. She recognizes and embraces that there are many different ways for a photographer to construct and expand their vision. With this spirit, she invites readers to go out in search of the unexpected and to give free rein to their dreams, memories, impressions, premonitions, ideas, and influences. She sees photography as part of a greater framework into which all the modes of human imagination can come together; the literature, film, architecture, art, and music we engage with enrich our lives and, in turn, our images.

Photography, Iturbide shows us, is a medium of expression forged by a combination of what is intuited within us and what is manifest in the world; of the surprise at what we see for the first time through our camera—what may even seem unfamiliar to us—and what is deeply our own. A memorable image is the result of the good luck that makes unexpected finds possible and the labor of introspection. The materiality of the world is just its starting point; a photograph is made through an individual, authorial interpretation.

Of course, none of these aspects can be reduced to a recipe that can be followed step-by-step. There is no method to be taught beyond a continued engagement with the medium, the world, and the self. Instead, through sharing her journey and inspirations as a photographer, Iturbide hopes to help those on the same quest find their own path.

Point of Contact

I think that all photographers are explorers. Photography is a pretext to know the world, to know life, to know yourself.

The way each one of us sees is different and is formed by what we have experienced, encountered, and learned as individuals; by what has nourished, surprised, and moved us; by the influences that have left traces in us, even unconsciously. Photographs emerge from both exterior realities and our inner selves—from within and from without. They cross our paths, but we also carry them. This is why I believe that photography is largely a matter of self-discovery. When I look at the images I have made, I see not only the fragments of the world I have been able to capture, often by chance, but also observe the imprint of my interpretations, projections, desires, and dreams. Thanks to photography, the world I have witnessed has allowed me to invent many other worlds fashioned by my sensibility that I then share with others.

There are countless ways that photography can be a source of creativity. Apart from inviting photographers to discover their own visions, I cannot extract practical lessons from my own work. Instead, I would like to give details about the context in which my images were made—about their connection to my own life. I'd like to reflect on their possible meanings as a way to share my experiences as a photographer. My photographs themselves contain more than I could ever possibly say, advise, or speculate about photography itself. Even after so many years as my medium of expression, photography never ceases to surprise me. It continues to give me a reason to learn about the world and myself.

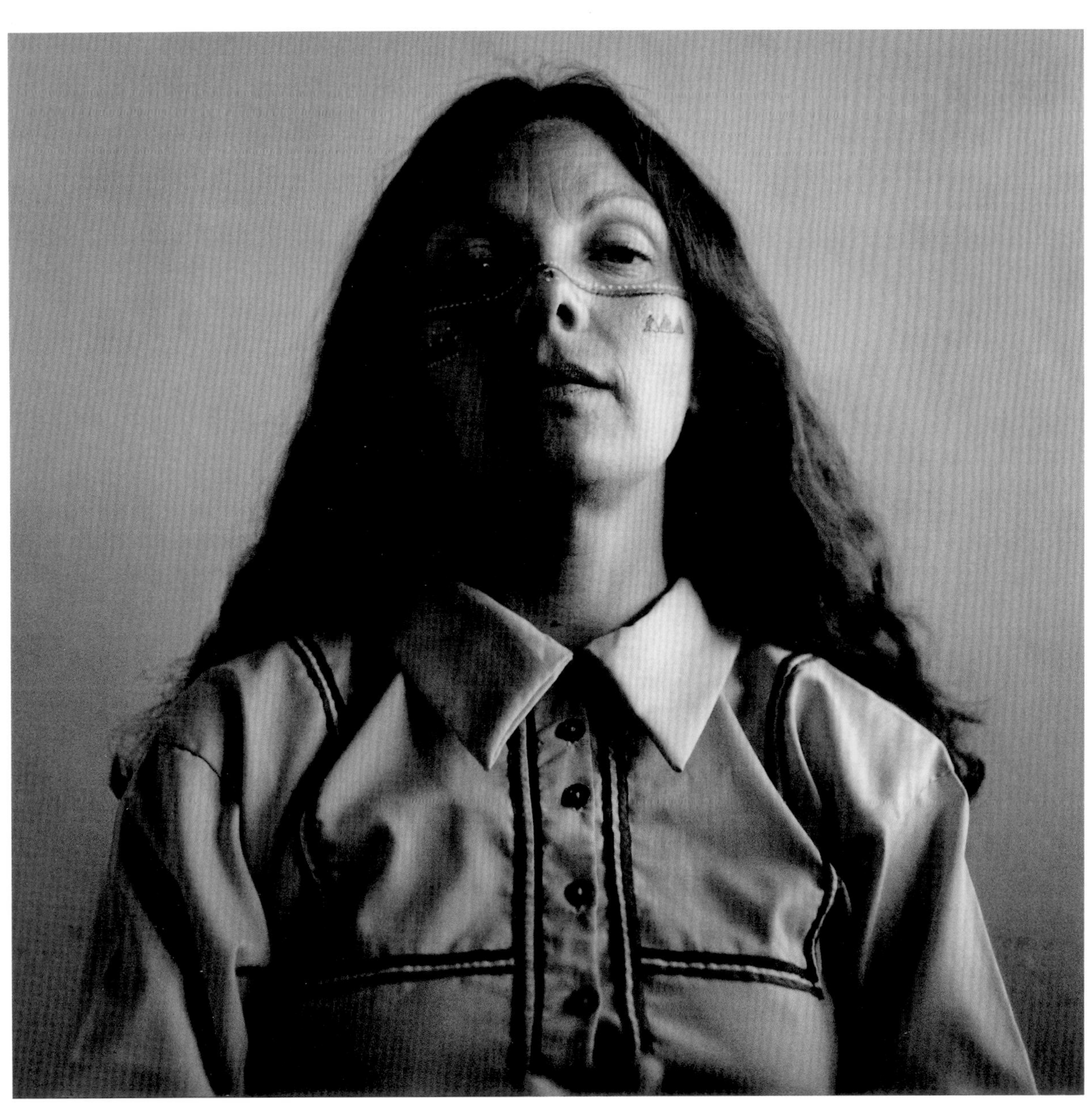

Graciela Iturbide
Autorretrato como Seri
(Self-portrait as Seri),
Sonoran Desert, Mexico, 1979

My father was an amateur photographer who made portraits of everyone in our family with a Rolleiflex camera. When I was a little girl, I discovered them in a tall chest of drawers in my parents' room, and they became my treasure. I loved to look at those prints, most of them small-format. I took the ones I liked best (without permission) and put them together in an album, mounting them on sheets of cardboard with photo corners. I gave some of the pictures away as a gift to the nuns at school. When this was discovered, I was scolded for rummaging in my parents' chest, and my album was broken up. That was my first encounter with the mysteries of photography.

When I was around eleven years old, my father gave me a Brownie camera, and I took my first pictures. He had them developed and printed at the same lab where he took his own film. I am still fond of the image I made of the little airplane I took to the boarding school where I was sent to study.

It is paradoxical that my fascination with photography began with me obsessively poring over family portraits taken by my father, who never looked kindly on my desire to express myself through an artistic discipline. Photography, whose spell bewitched me, was to become, years later, a way of freeing myself from that world of conservative values to which he and many members of my family ascribed. In a lot of my work, you find the echoes of the Catholic Church: angels, crosses, all of the things I lived with as a girl. Though I'm not a believer, those influences are still there. We may reject our upbringing, but we carry it with us; it is part of us.

One of my brothers recently sent me photographs that my father had taken before he was married. Those scratched and wrinkled negatives show the places he lived, worked, and visited. There are images of archaeological sites and the ruins of Mitla; of my father next to a tiger; of women I never knew but whose appearance intrigue me. One of my future projects is to publish these photos, which vaguely recall the life of a man who was not yet my father. Photography is once more, as in the days when I rummaged through the chest of drawers, our point of contact.

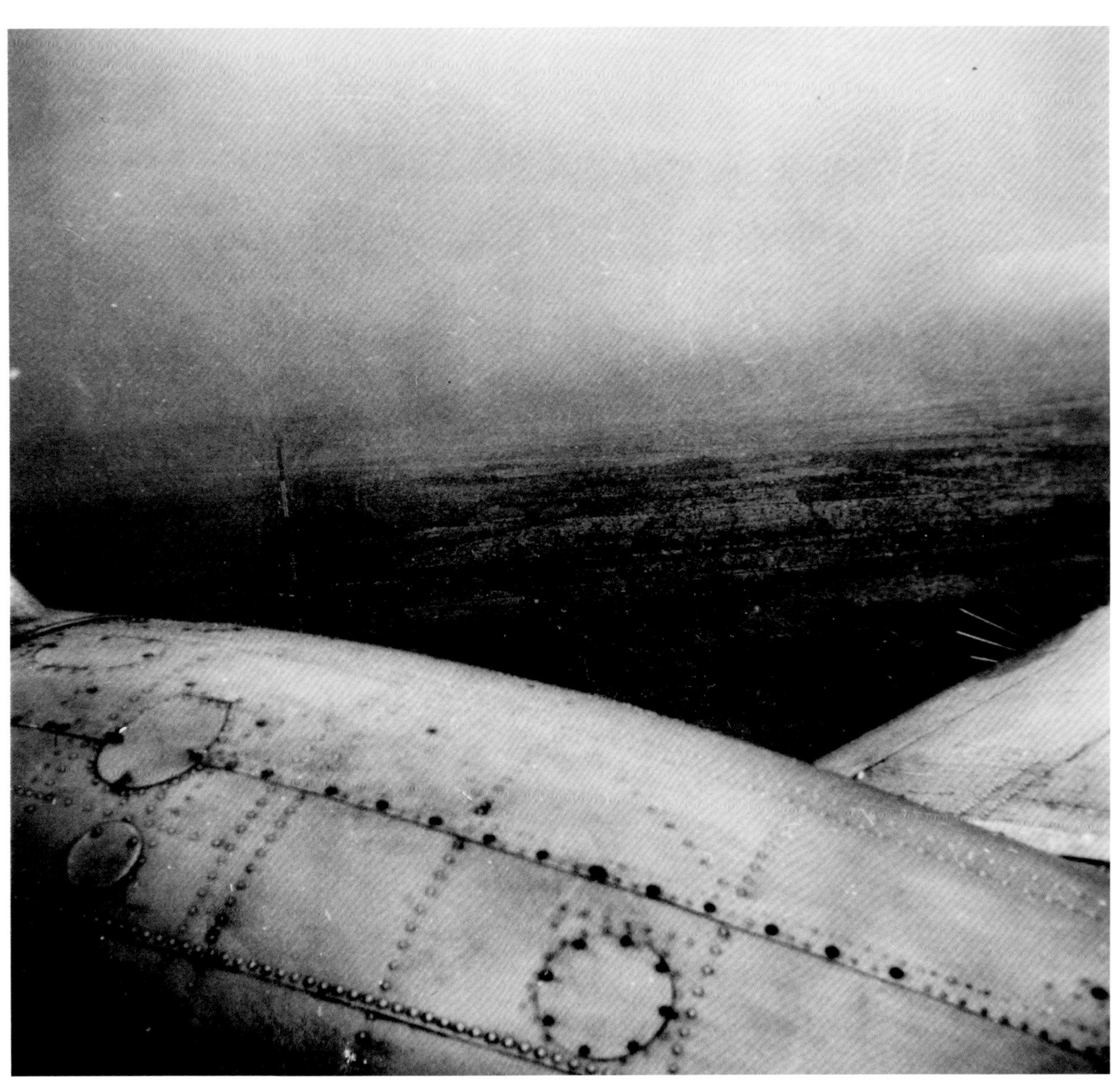

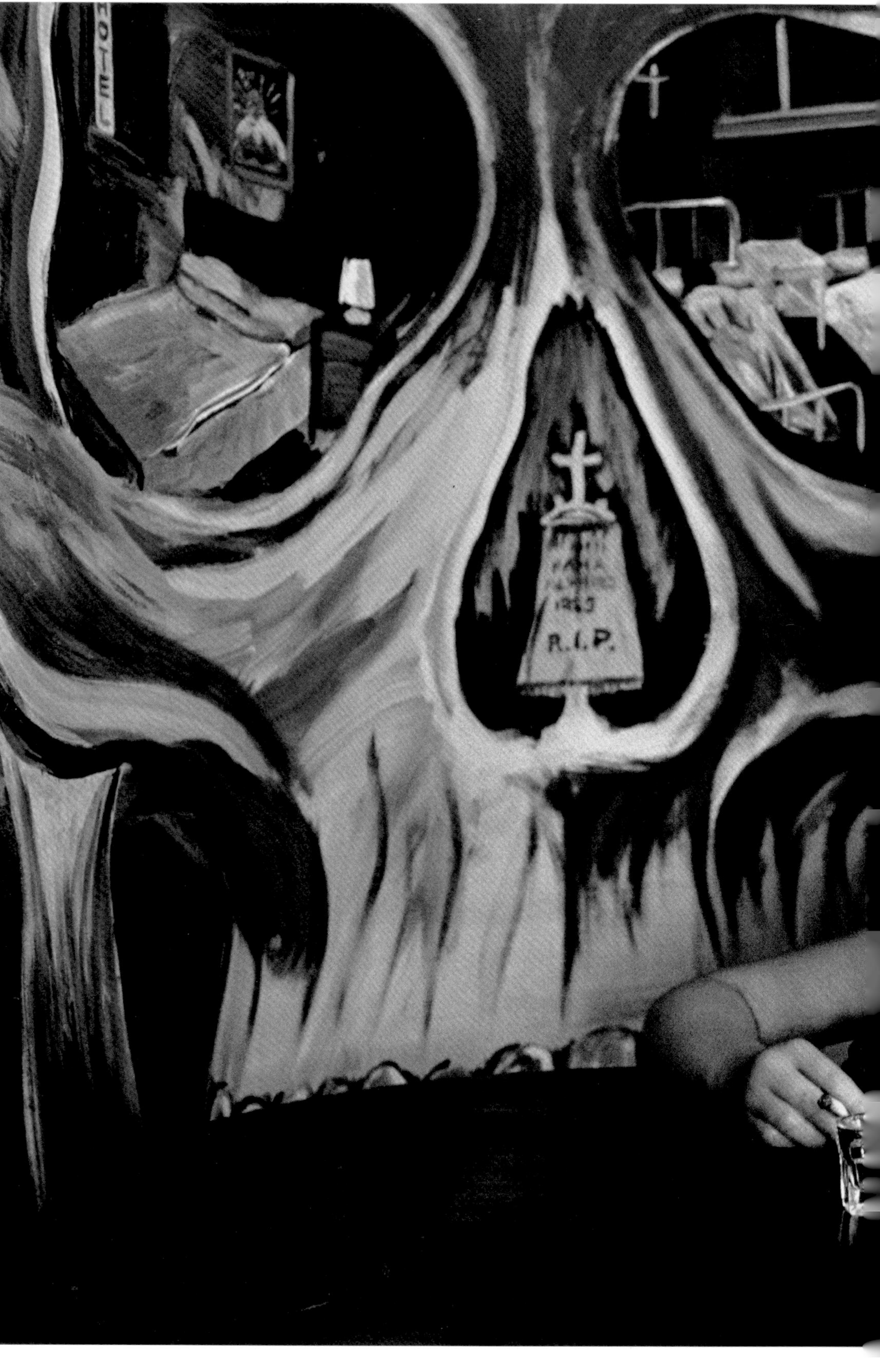
HOTEL
R.I.P.

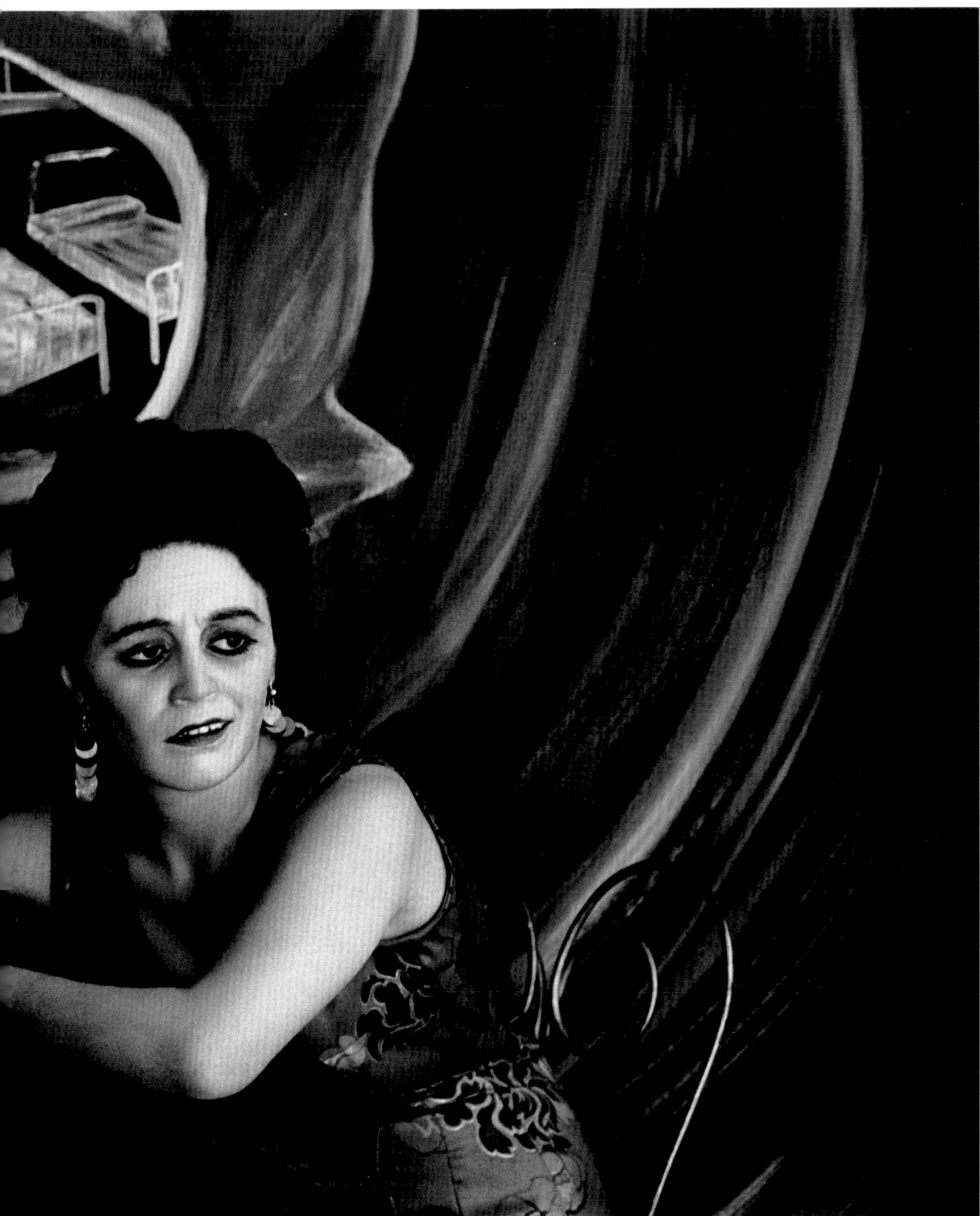

Like Magic

I was older than most other students when I entered the Universidad Nacional Autónoma de México to study film. I was already married and had children. I had heard by chance about the film school and was so eager to do something with my life that I enrolled. Images had always appealed to me, but it had never occurred to me to study film. When I was a girl, I wanted to become a writer or to study philosophy, but my very conservative upbringing wouldn't allow that. The father of my children was a more liberal man. In my day, it was unusual for husbands to say, "Yes, yes, of course, go study."

As luck would have it, I met Manuel Álvarez Bravo. Almost no one took his classes because they all wanted to be movie directors, but I happened to have one of his books, a catalogue that I picked up at the Lagunilla flea market for a retrospective exhibition that took place during the 1968 Olympics in Mexico City. I approached him to sign the book and to ask if I could sit in on his class, which was a higher-level course. Not only did he allow me to take the class but immediately offered to make me his *achichincle*, or apprentice. (In Mexico, an *achichincle* is a carpenter's or mason's assistant.) I could hardly believe it. I think he picked up on the excitement I felt at seeing his images. I had good teachers in the film school, but there was something about still photography that attracted me. Film is like a novel, while photography is like a poem.

More than teaching me about photography, Manuel Álvarez Bravo taught me about the life of an artist. He never told me whether my photographs were good or bad—never. But he spoke to me a lot about painting, about literature. We listened to Bach in the afternoons. He instilled in me a poetic sense of time and timelessness, so Mexican in nature, that was also his own. He used to say, "Graciela, there is no need to hurry, there is time. Don't hurry to exhibit. You have a lot of work to do."

I would go out with my camera and take pictures of everything. Manuel would say, "Chaca chaca chaca chaca, why so much junk, Graciela? For what?" He almost always took one photograph. If, by chance, he took two, it was already too many. I don't know how he did it. I remember one trip where he only brought one roll of 35 mm film.

When I come across something I like, I might take three or four photographs in case one turns out blurry, but I'm not a compulsive photographer. I learned a more thoughtful way of taking photographs from Álvarez Bravo.

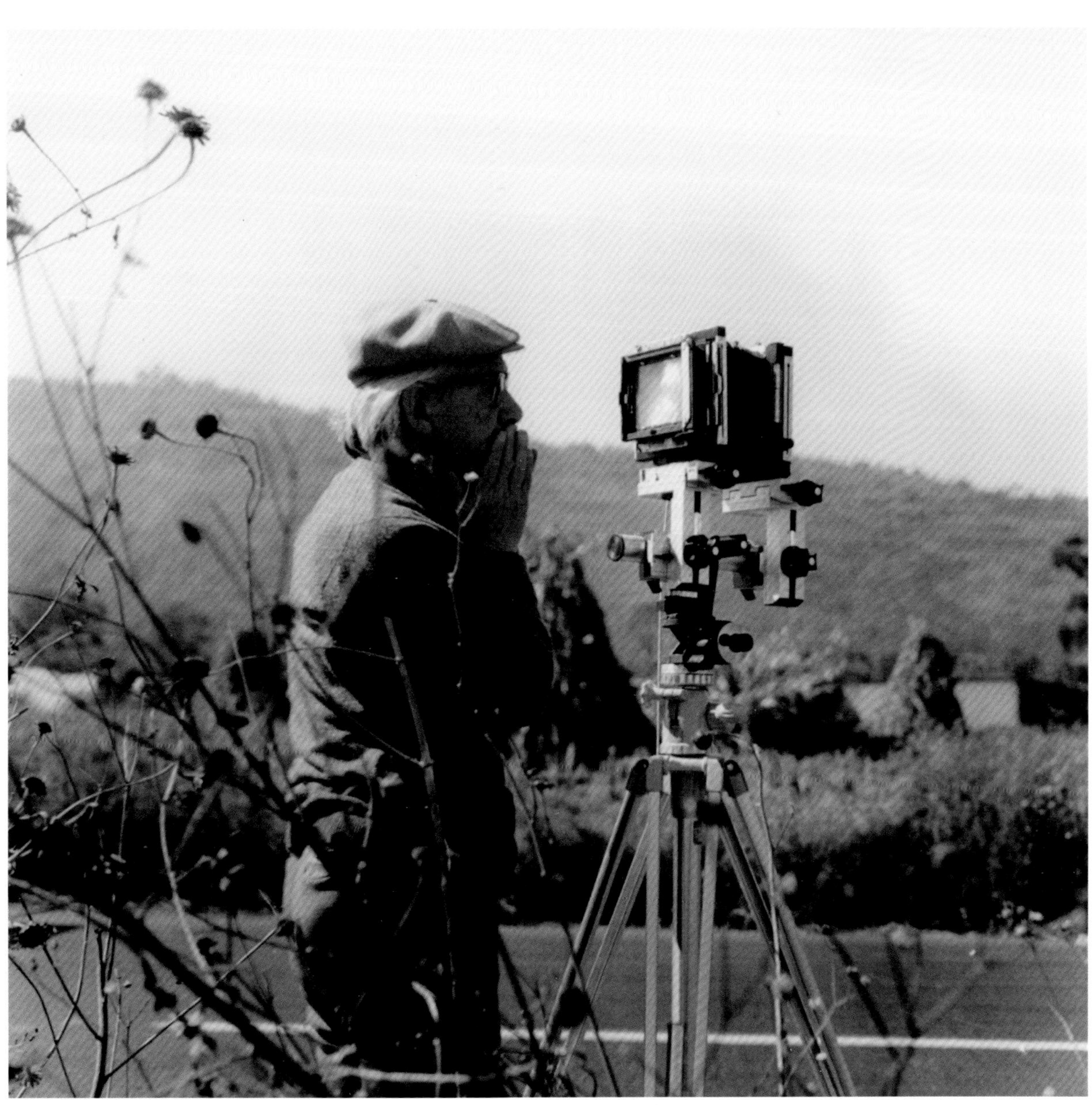

Graciela Iturbide
Manuel Álvarez Bravo, 1970

I was lucky that when I began to work with him, the Museum of Modern Art in New York had asked him to make prints of Tina Modotti's work: he had known Modotti well and was able to interpret her negatives. Álvarez Bravo was not someone who focused on perfect mastery of technique. He would point out the beauty of a black tone or the different shades of gray, but he was not a perfectionist, like Ansel Adams. Let's just say that Manuel Álvarez Bravo relied more on intuition, on feeling more than reason. I once asked him, "Maestro, how do you properly develop a roll of black-and-white film?" He responded, "You know, Graciela, go to the store, buy yourself a roll of film, and read the instructions. That's how you do it." In his wisdom, he wanted me to start working and exploring for myself rather than getting caught up in technicalities. For me to watch how the blacks and grays developed in the darkroom was something that seemed, in that moment, like magic.

His way of seeing the world fascinated me—the presence of the pre-Hispanic world in his work, the influence of folk art. His home was full of little figurines that we would buy in Mexican villages; he had great respect for the traditional artist. Seeing and getting to know Mexico through his eyes influenced me immeasurably.

At the same time, he used to tell me that influences were necessary, but it was just as necessary to suppress them and acquire one's own language. After a year and a half, I felt it was time to cut the cord, to set out on my own.

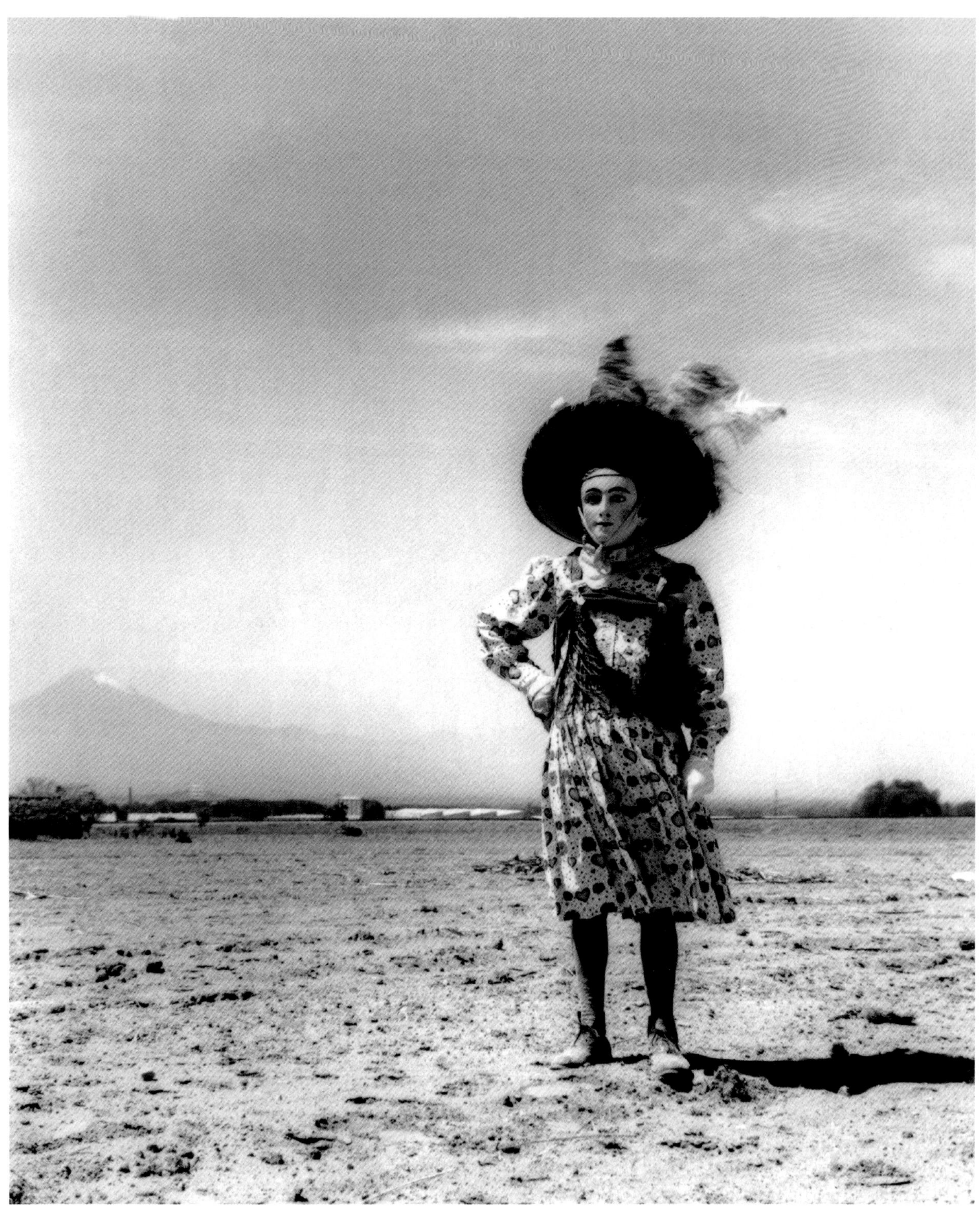

Graciela Iturbide
Carnaval (Carnival),
Tlaxcala, Mexico, 1974

There have been times along the way when I've had money and times I haven't.
But even when I didn't have money, there were rolls of film in my refrigerator.
When I first got started, I had the help of my husband; when I got divorced, the
only work I could find was for magazines like *Mundo médico* (Medical world)
and *Médico moderno* (Modern doctor) photographing operations. I took
photographs of people who asked me to take their photograph: lots of portraits,
even weddings. I managed. But I never stopped taking my own photographs.

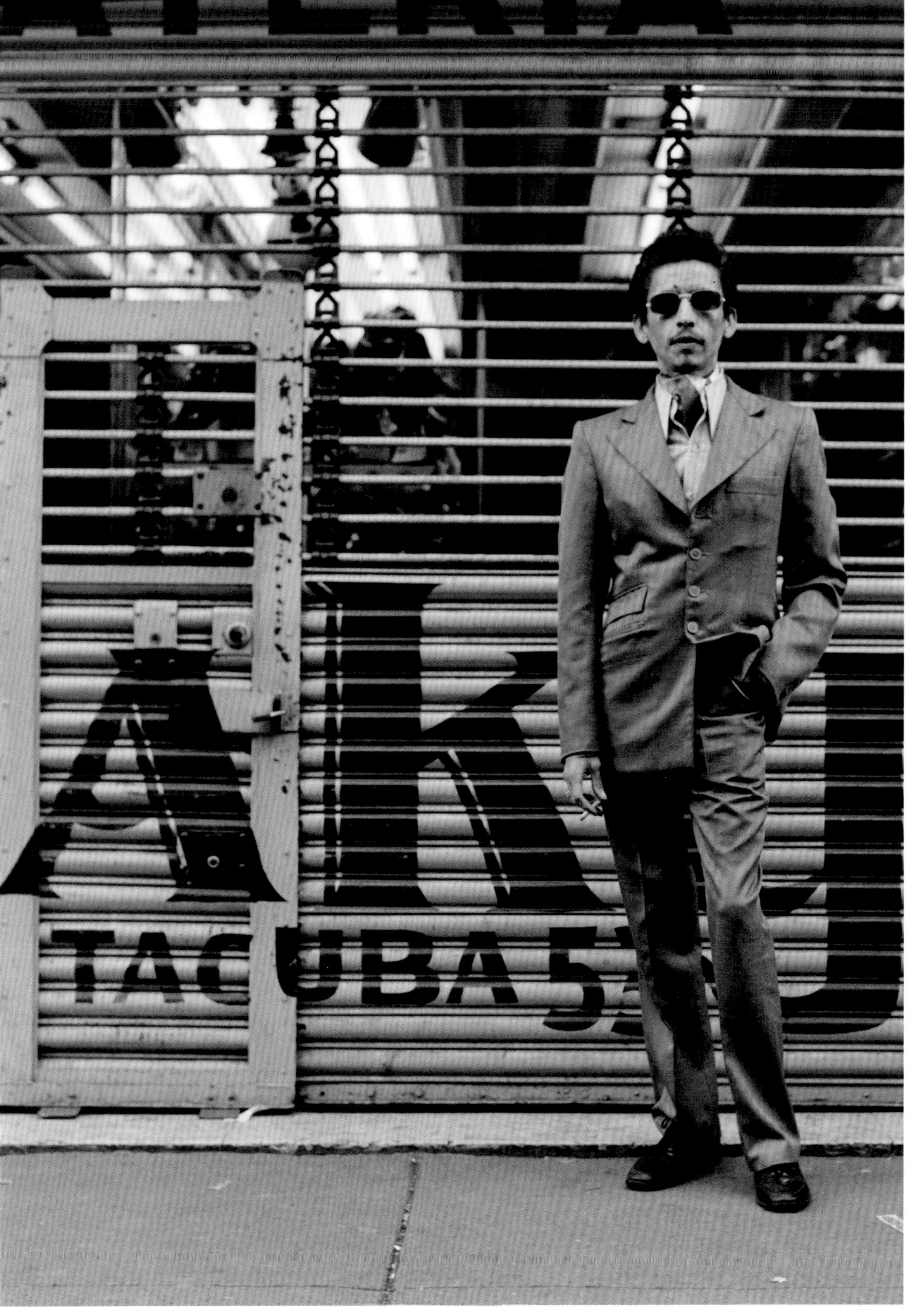

TACUBA 5

Mexico City, and above all its historic center, was the scene of my own explorations, where I made the images I consider my first works of photography. There was always something to capture my attention in that urban space, where large numbers of people, a diversity of cultural expressions, and all kinds of activities come together, and where the different strata of history are still visible.

Photography helps me, above all, to see: it forces me to pay more attention to details whenever I am busy following the action. Mexico City—whose streets I continue to explore on foot—has shown me that the ordinary is the real source of the extraordinary. Street photography reveals to me how marvels are concealed within the commonplace. Of course, I'm predisposed to think this way, having had the good fortune to be born Mexican, to belong to a country where the legends of pre-Hispanic cultures still pervade our daily lives. Capturing the symbolism and meaning—the poetic dimension of humankind—is what most interests me, rather than exercises in photographic style.

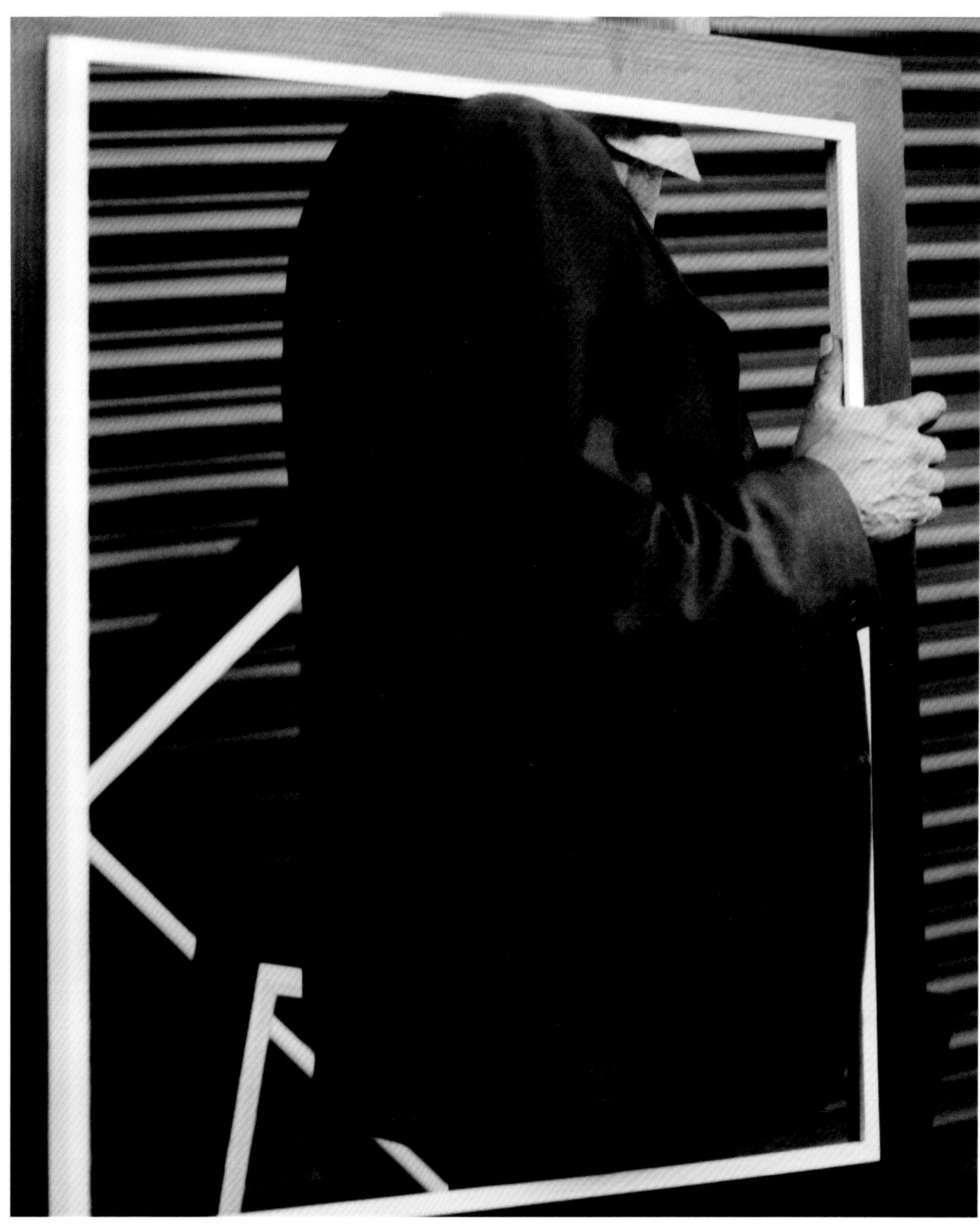

Graciela Iturbide
Señor enmarcado (Framed man),
Mexico City, 1972

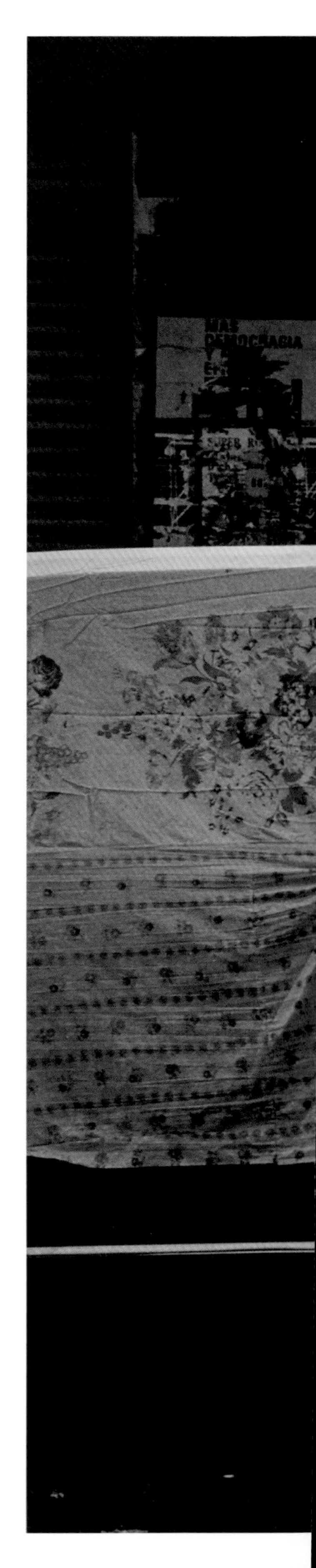

Graciela Iturbide
Carro (Car), Tepito,
Mexico City, 1972

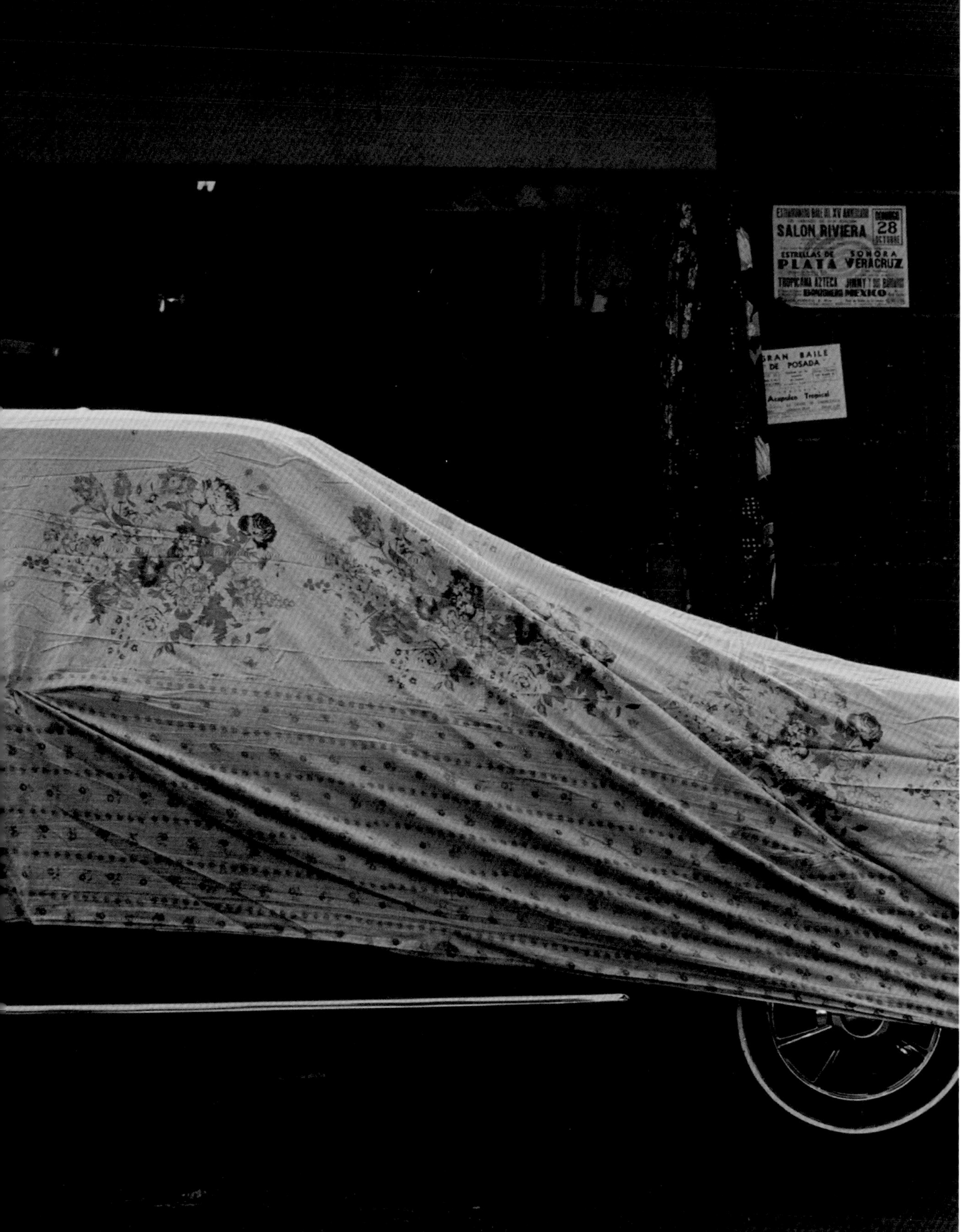
SALON RIVIERA
28
OCTUBRE
ESTRELLAS DE   SONORA
PLATA VERACRUZ
TROPICANA AZTECA
MEXICO
GRAN BAILE
DE POSADA
Acapulco Tropical

Everything You Carry

My photographs are a companion to the reality of the situation. You could say that my eyes see, but my heart photographs.

What you see through a lens, what catches your eye and causes you to point a camera, is highly subjective. Without the camera, you see the world in one way, and with it, another. Photography is not truth. Photographers interpret what is in front of them. Through this little window you compose, even dream, the reality in front of you. Even though you are seeing what passes before your lens for the first time, what the eye perceives is a synthesis of who you are, what you have learned: that is the photographic language. The task of the photographer is to infuse what we see with who we are, to make poetry out of reality.

The way that I photograph is very intuitive; I never consciously worked to develop a style. As I learned from Álvarez Bravo, photography is basically everything that surrounds you: what you read, what you see. We look at so many images now, in advertising, on television, in the media. I have found that in order to work at my own rhythm, I need to put those images aside to cultivate my intuition and be singular in my vision.

A photographer without imagination is not a good photographer; neither is one whose pictures are too self-conscious and mannered. That kills a picture for me. You have to be attuned to your intuition, but it should be invisible in your photographs. The eye must capture everything you carry within you very quickly.

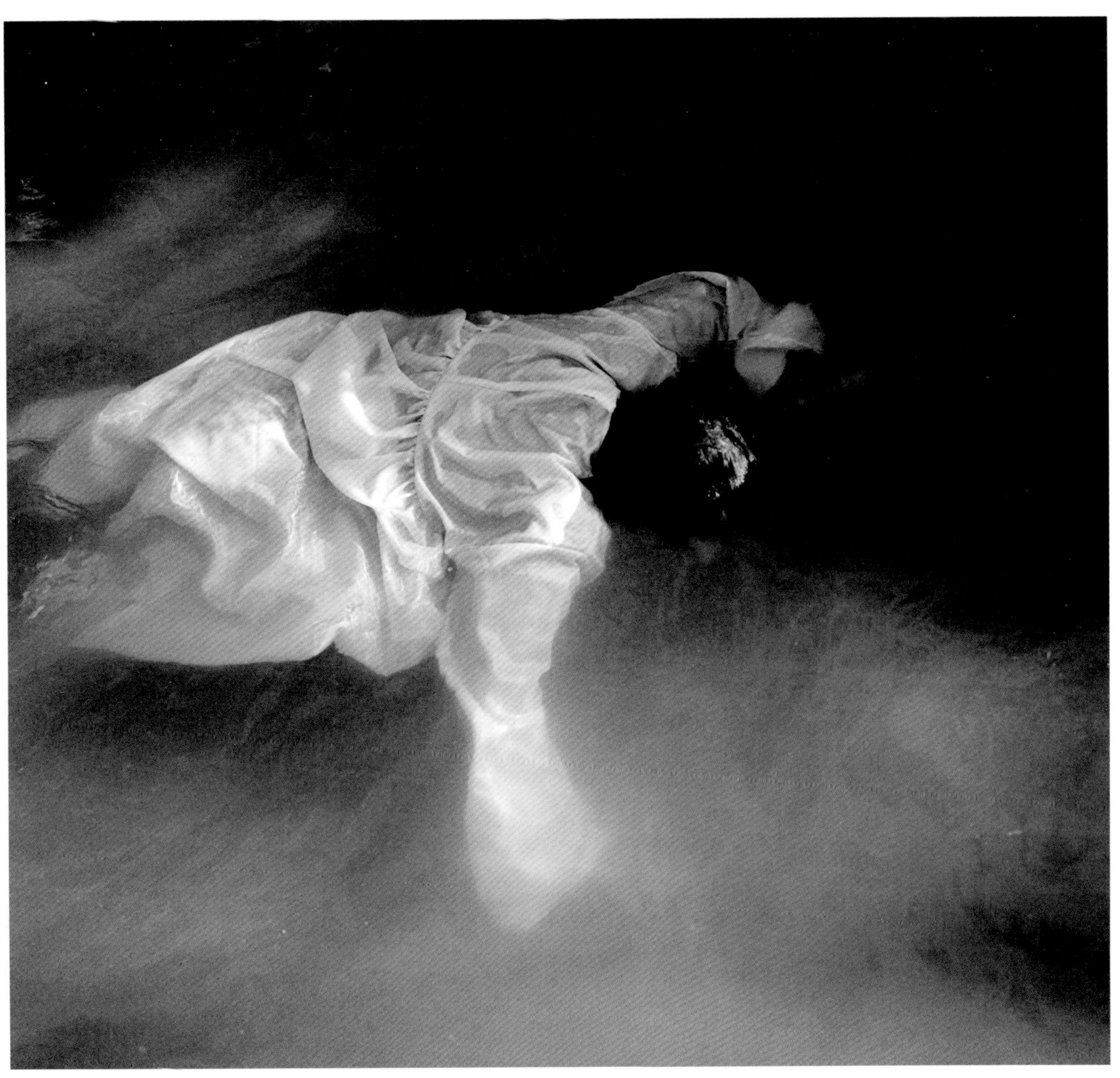

Graciela Iturbide
Ritual, Fiesta del Niño Fidencio
(Ritual, Niño Fidencio Festival),
Espinazo, Nuevo Leon, Mexico, 2000

Chance is a fundamental component of my photography and even, I might say, of my life. Many of my images are the result of unexpected encounters, of unforeseen occurrences, of accidents, of everything summed up in the word *serendipity*.

I enjoy discovering what life puts before my eyes with the help of the camera. Everything comes to me on its own—all I have to do is be ready to receive it. Because the extraordinary can become visible at any moment, but only to those who remain attentive, I have learned to wait, to be patient, to fit into the different rhythms of the worlds that I photograph.

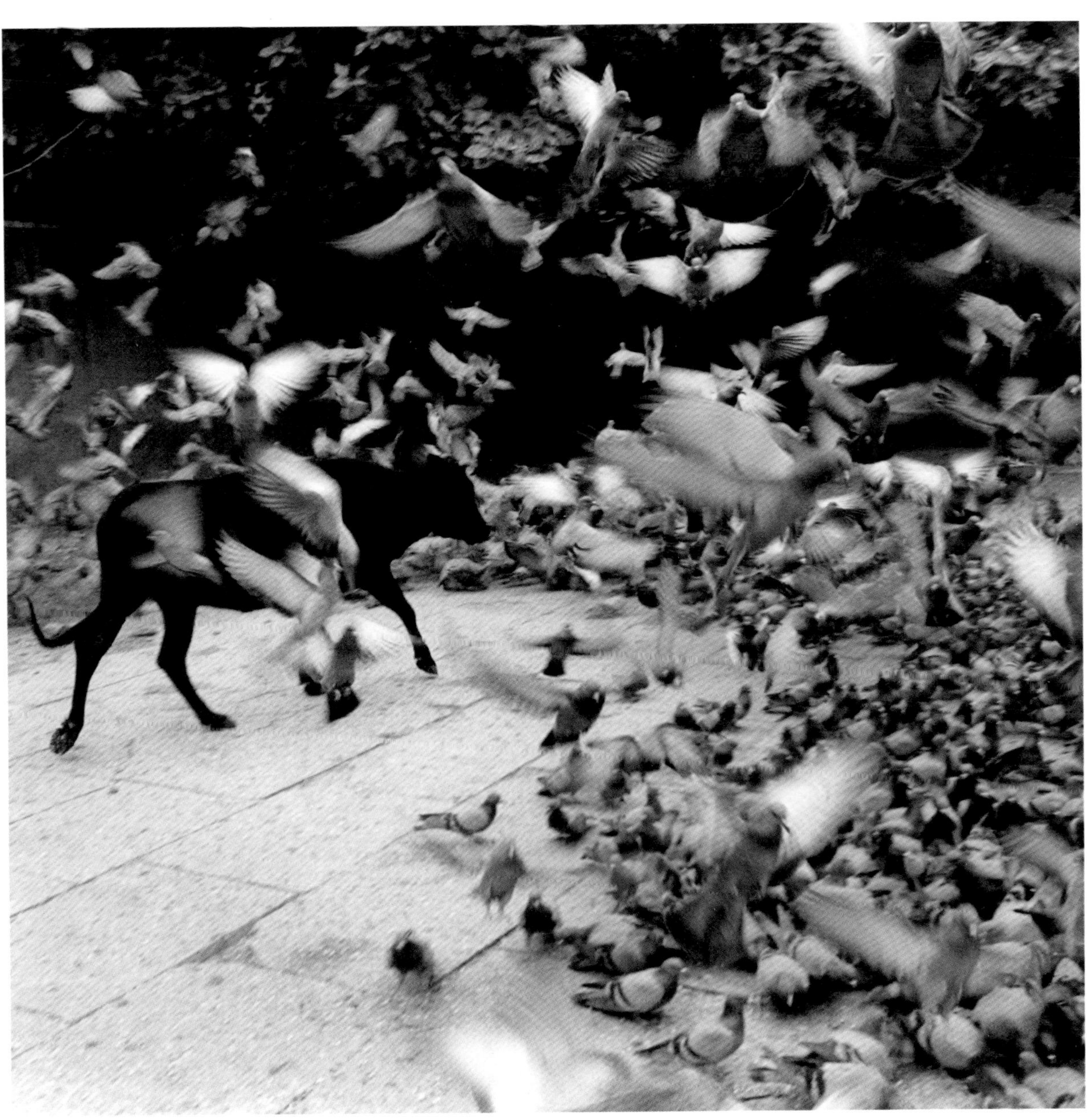

Graciela Iturbide
Untitled, Jaipur, India, 1999

It's never clear to me what I want to photograph, even when I'm asked to photograph something specific. Surprise is what gets me to take a picture. If I say, "Ay! What a wonder!" I press the shutter.

Your training and your instincts are working subconsciously in the background all the time, but surprise is instantaneous. I may be in a garden or at a fiesta: Why do I stop at a certain point when there are a hundred possible places to stop? Because I sense something amazing at work there. I cannot photograph if a spark of wonder is not ignited. The spark that animates my photographs can be found anywhere: in people, buildings, landscapes, things; in rituals and in everyday life; in any action or event. This is why I have photographed in all genres—categories are just different ways of appreciating the richness of reality. Everything is related.

I take photographs for the pleasure of being amazed and to keep a record of what surprises me. If you think about photographing in this way, it becomes a much more selective process from beginning to end, rather than one of simply catching, catching, catching without much thought in order to find a worthwhile picture in a pile of images later.

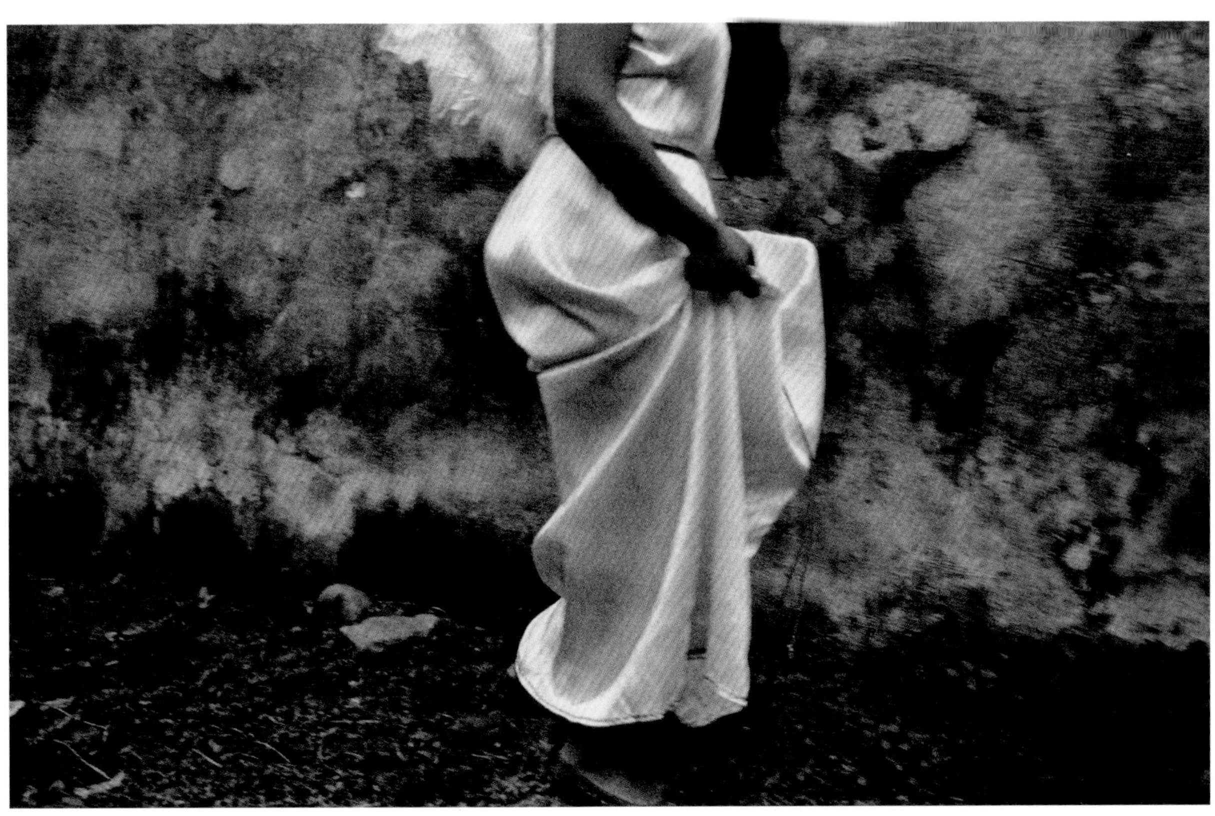

29

Those We Are Still Looking For

"I want the photos I take to be an immediate experience, not something ruminated over. Nevertheless, I know that photography, like any art, must be pursued within oneself. The perfect photograph is like a miracle. It takes place in an instant of light, forms, subject matter, and a perfect state of mind: you press a button almost without realizing it, and the miracle occurs." These are the words of the Chilean photographer Sergio Larraín, one of my most illustrious predecessors. But for a miracle to take place, you have to know how to sacrifice.

You may think that a photographer must never miss the moment, or any opportunity for a good image, "the eye of a lynx and a silk glove," as Henri Cartier-Bresson put it. Nothing could be more untrue. The ability to hold back and not make a photograph is indispensable in order to avoid transforming the camera into an instrument of aggression. This kind of waiting also ensures you'll never be satisfied with a mediocre result: it teaches you to insist on the best and the most beautiful. Though you will also miss once-in-a-lifetime moments.

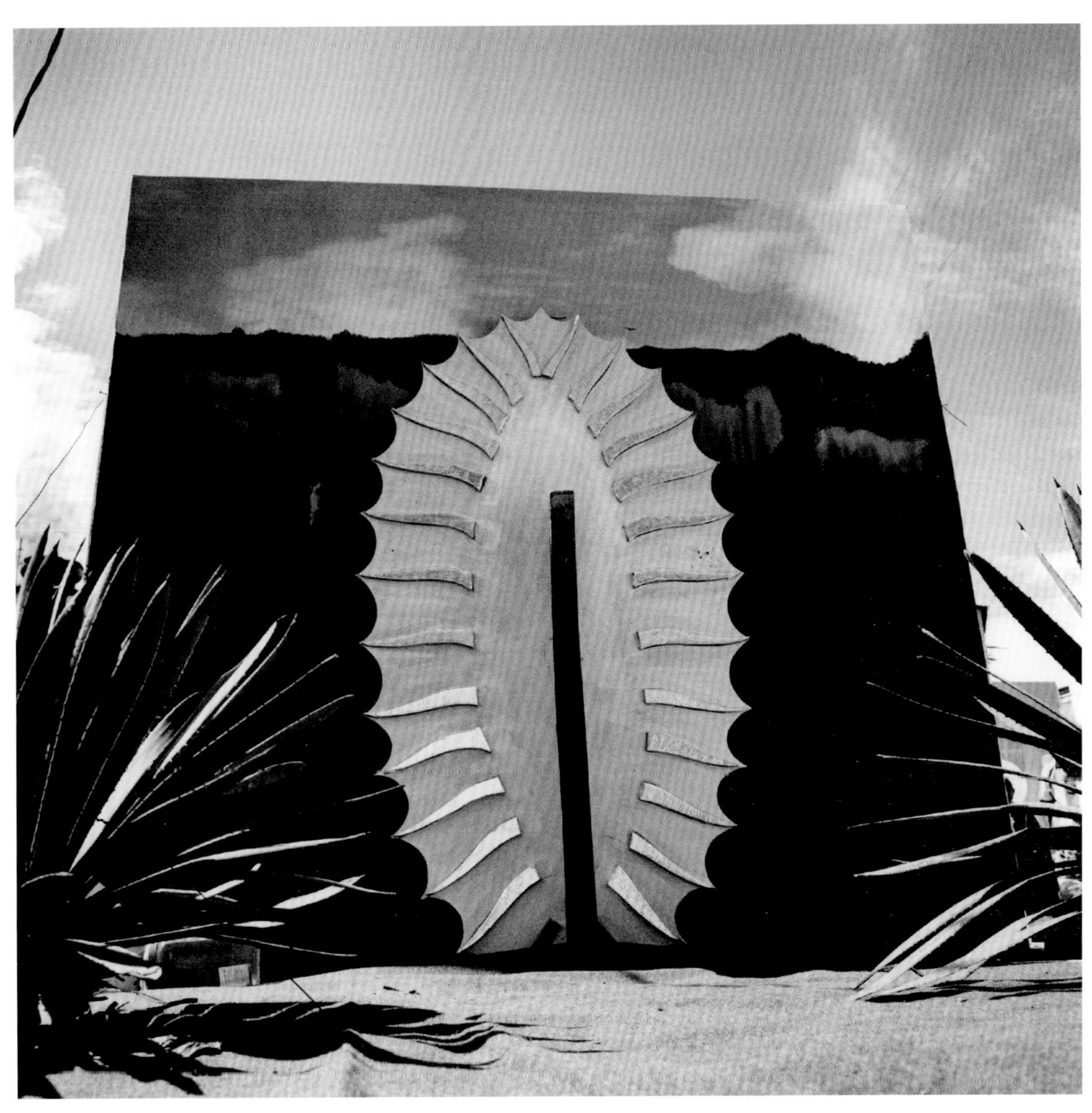

Graciela Iturbide
Virgen de Guadalupe
(Virgin of Guadalupe),
Chalma, Mexico, 2008

For many, the "decisive moment" is the most important thing—the photographer
anticipates the peak moment within the constant flow of life and captures it in a frac-
tion of a second. But when I'm photographing, I'm more obsessed with composition
than with timing. I spotted this scene in Tlaxcala: upside-down chickens seemed
very strange to me! At the time, I was so focused on making this almost abstract
photo that when a couple of newlyweds passed by, with one of their mothers trailing
behind them, I was so taken aback that I failed to take the picture. I have regretted
missing that picture my whole life. It was a Pier Paolo Pasolini vision in Mexico—the
dust of Tlaxcala, the bride with her veil next to the bicycle. I could have shouted,
"Wait a second!" or tried to take the picture very quickly, but I missed my chance.
That gorgeous image, full of pathos, escaped me. The photograph might have come
out unfocused, or maybe the whole thing was just my imagination, influenced by
Pasolini or Fellini films. My eye and imagination were alert, but even so I was unable
to capture the moment that the world offered me. Perhaps I lack the lynx's eye.

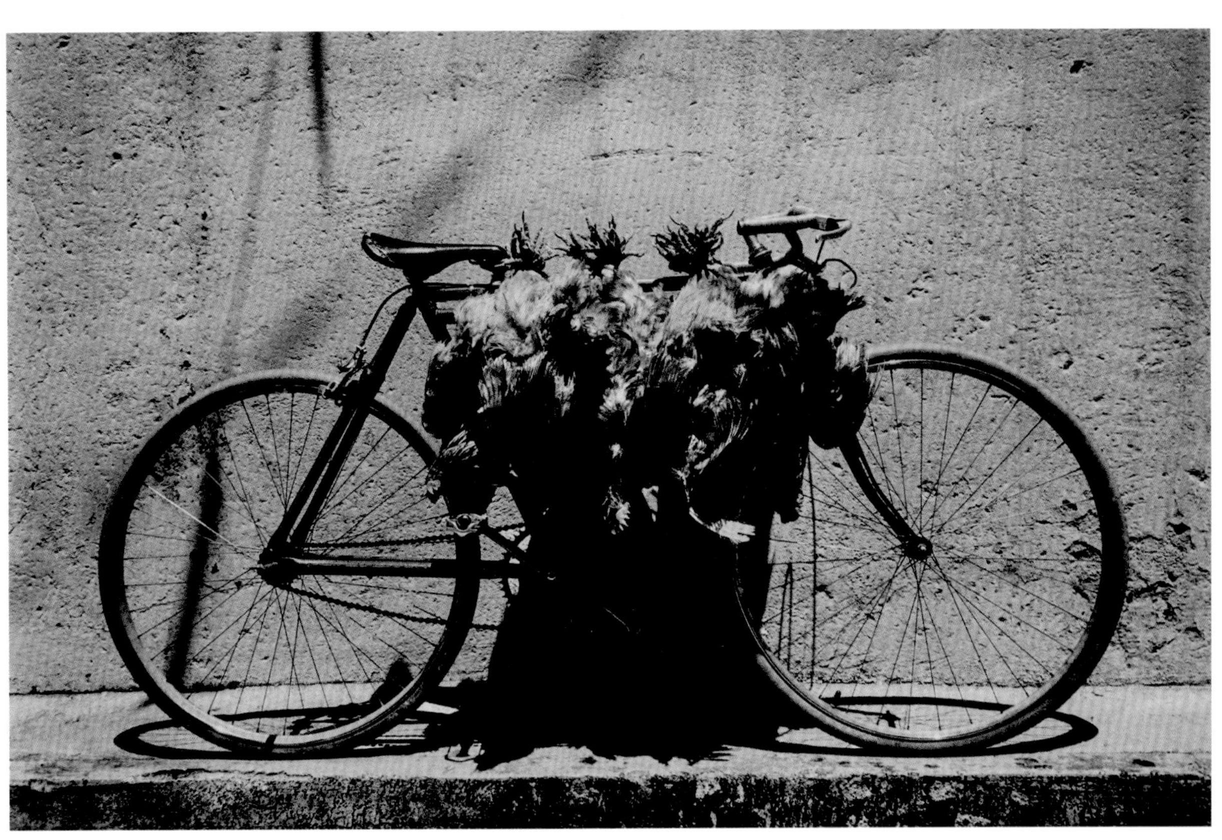

Graciela Iturbide
El viaje (The voyage),
Tlaxcala, Mexico, 1995

I adore the ritual of photography: to go out with the camera to observe the most mythological aspects of people, and then go into the darkness to develop the most symbolic images.

After the decisive moment of taking a picture comes another no-less-defining decision: reviewing your images to select the most successful ones—separating them from those that are just alright or almost there. Only in this "second decisive moment" do I discover my images. You think that you took one photo, but another comes out. Sometimes a picture you had little hope for ends up being a pleasant surprise. To be a photographer means not only clicking the shutter but knowing how to look at your images and recognize what speaks to you.

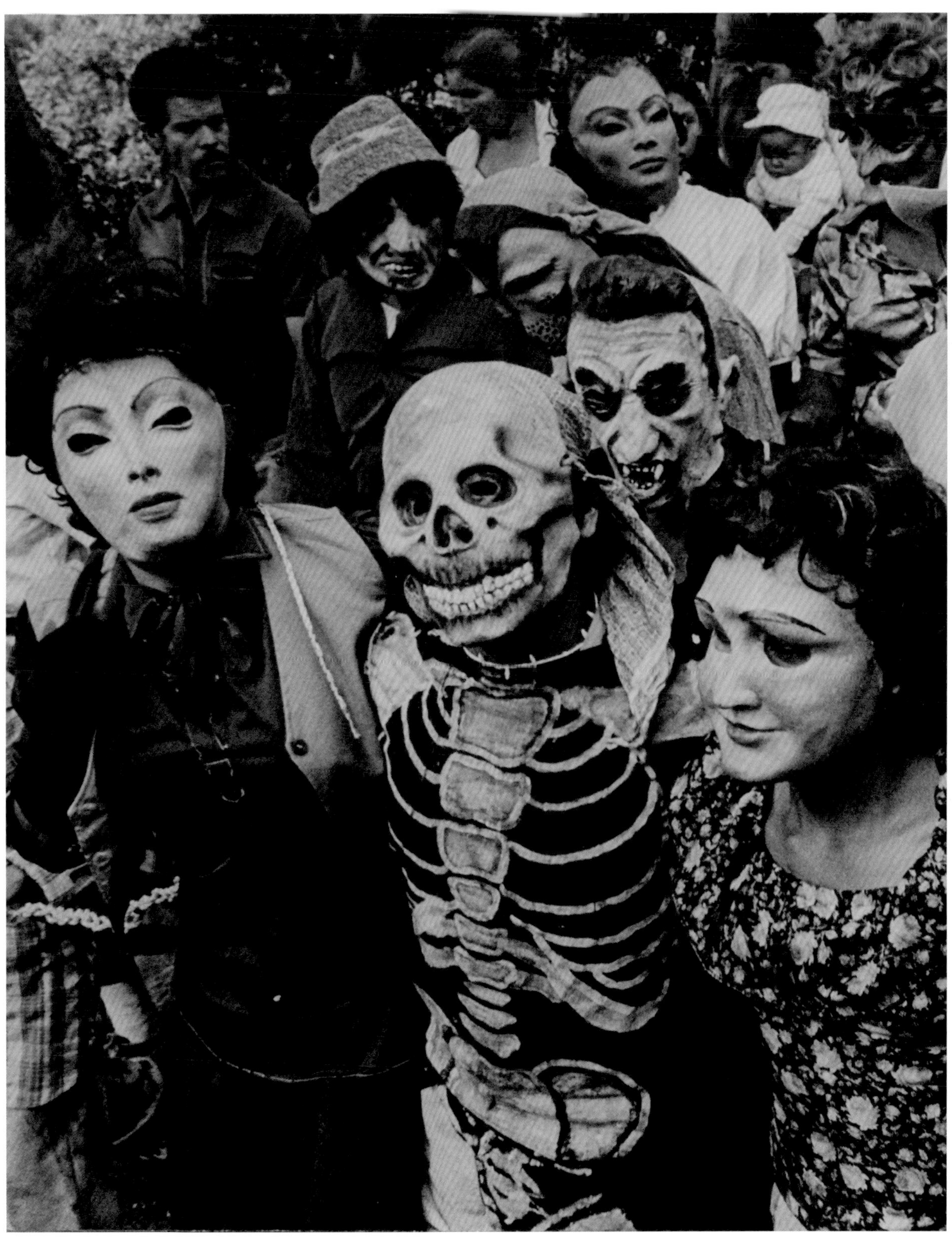

Graciela Iturbide
Procesión (Procession),
Chalma, Mexico, 1984

Other photographers have called me a hopeless romantic because I continue to use film. The contact sheet is how I best evaluate and reevaluate my work; I don't have this relationship with digital files. For me, photography is a ritual. When I return home from a journey, I develop my photographs and lay out my contact sheets. I then put them away. After some time has passed, I take them out again to make a selection, knowing my vision will change over time.

I didn't print from the negative of the woman hurrying past a wall at first, because she was out of focus. In looking at it over time, I realized that didn't matter. The focus of attention is on the paint stains, which appear to be blood. It took eight years for this image to come out of my contact sheets.

When I work in 6-by-6, I usually print two contact sheets for each roll of film. I cut one of them up and lay the images on a table, arranging them into different series and sequences. I like to play around with images, even if it takes me down paths I don't ultimately follow. I then make small prints that I tack onto the wall, and finally, I make choices based on a theme. Preparing for a book or an exhibition, especially, gives me the opportunity to reactivate and renew my archive.

We photographers learn from our own images, which are endowed with a life of their own. They help us to understand our interest in certain subjects, to appreciate the affinities and particularities of our compositions, and to start to form sets or series. Our earlier work informs our ongoing practice. A continuity exists between the images we have already taken and those we are still looking for.

Graciela Iturbide
Los pollos (Chickens),
Juchitán, Oaxaca, Mexico, 1979

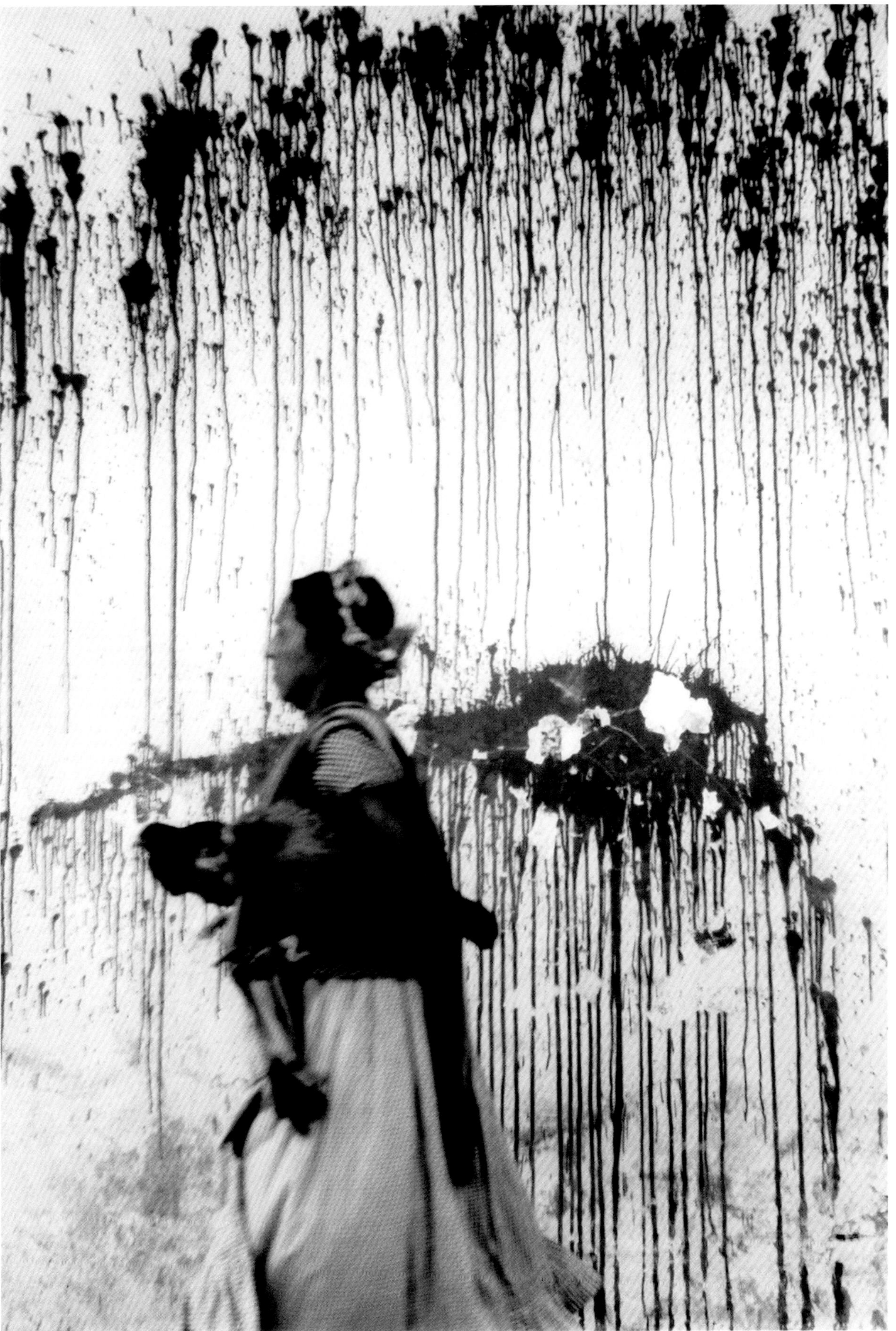

My Eye

When I photograph in black and white, I see in black and white. When I photograph in color, I see in color. My mind adjusts to the necessities and possibilities of each.

I have worked in color on commission and often photograph in color as a tool for gathering samples of graphic material—traces of urban writing that have faded with time: signs, announcements, logos, letter-forms—in tandem with documenting a subject. I have never made much use of the large number of slides and Polaroids in my archive, though I have thought about publishing my "working" Polaroids as Walker Evans did.

For the most part, I work in black and white, with analog techniques, in prints of modest dimensions. I even dream in black and white sometimes.

Color photography reminds me of Disneyland. It seems to me that when someone photographs in color in places like Mexico or India, already so colorful on their own, the images run the risk of falling into exoticism or sensationalism. At the same time, I greatly admire the color photography of Miguel Rio Branco, William Eggleston, and Mary Ellen Mark. Manuel Álvarez Bravo took some color images that I think are very successful, and I find the Polaroids of Andrei Tarkovsky fascinating. I consider Pablo López Luz's color work remarkable, and in Anna Malagrida's photographs, I like the way that color gradually blurs into white.

For me, black-and-white images retain the mystery that exists in what we see. Photographing in black and white is an exercise in abstraction from the moment that you point the camera—it helps remove the harshness of reality, so to speak. As Octavio Paz wrote in "Cara al tiempo" (Facing time), the poem he dedicated to Álvarez Bravo: "Reality is more real in black and white."

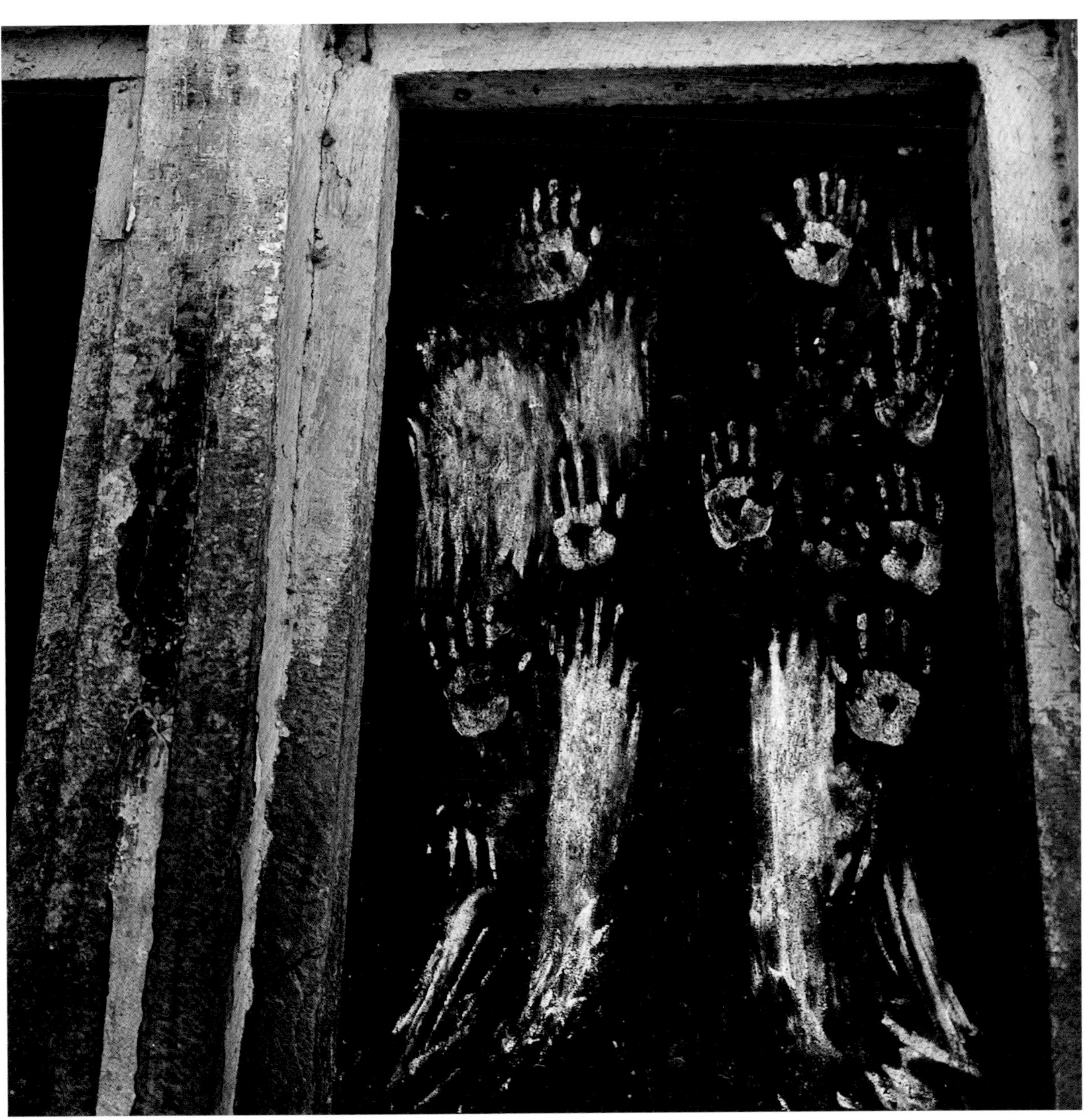

Graciela Iturbide
Untitled, Varanasi, India, 1997

I like to experiment with how images are presented if a project allows for it (or demands it). I have painted on or scratched up some of my images just for fun. I don't adhere to any orthodoxy regarding the publication or presentation of my images. I like to stay open to new possibilities.

I wanted to make a book that would bring together a more personal selection of photographs from my archive, chosen because they have a certain mystery to them. My original idea was to call it *Mal de ojo* (Evil eye). I began working with publisher Editorial RM and it ended up being titled *Mi ojo* (My eye) instead, at the suggestion of publisher Ramón Reverté and designer Estela Robles, who was superstitious. They also came up with the idea of printing the images in silver ink on black paper so that they appear as ghostly negatives on the page. I loved the mock-up they prepared, which was inspired by Japanese book design and used my own handwriting for the title on the cover, lifted from a note I sent to Estela's husband, artist Frederic Amat. In the end, the published book almost exactly matched the mock-up.

This often happens with books and exhibitions that are collaborative efforts: the original ideas are modified and enriched by the creativity of other people.

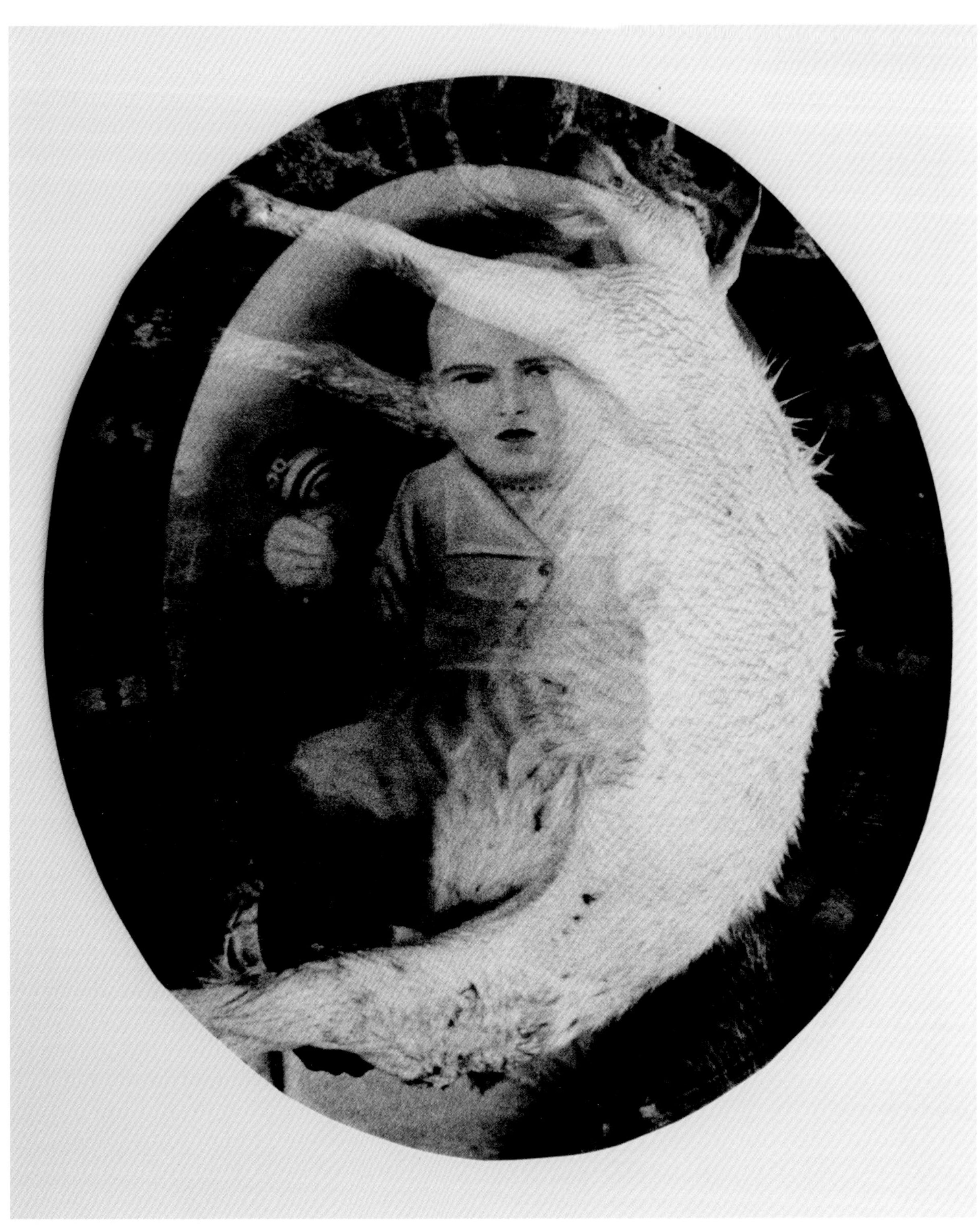

Graciela Iturbide
Retrato de familia (Family portrait),
La Mixteca, Oaxaca, Mexico, 1992

Encounters

One of the reasons I became a photographer was to get to know my country and its diverse cultures.

I visited Juchitán for the first time during Easter Week of 1979. The town is located on the Isthmus of Tehuantepec in southern Mexico, a region that has been inhabited by Zapotec peoples for thousands of years. Part of the state of Oaxaca, its cultural and ethnographic riches are renowned. As with other places in Oaxaca, the myths, language, and traditions of the Indigenous past remain alive among the people, even as they adapt to new ways of life.

The painter Francisco Toledo had seen my work and invited me to take photographs of Juchitán, where he was from. He and a group of local artists had founded the town's Casa de la Cultura five years before, and whatever images I took would contribute to its holdings and be published in a book. At that time, Juchitán was also the scene of a grassroots movement against the anti-democratic administrations of the Partido Revolucionario Institucional (Mexico's longtime ruling party), led by the Coalition of Workers, Campesinos, and Students of the Isthmus (COCEI in Spanish). Toledo got many artists and intellectuals to support this organization. I didn't know, when I met Toledo for the first time at a café in Mexico City, that I would end up photographing in Juchitán for the next ten years.

Thanks to Toledo's friends and relatives, it was easy for me to connect with the people of Juchitán. Macario Matus, a poet and the director of Casa de la Cultura, was one of the guides who helped open doors for me. Before too long, the *juchitecos*, especially the women, got to know me, and I began to make friends. This was important to my being able to photograph. I went everywhere with my camera so that people would know that I was a photographer, and I also lived with them, which created solidarity. People were happy to have their portraits taken as they went about their daily activities or celebrated their fiestas. At first, I stayed in a cheap hotel near the market. As I made friends, I started staying at Serafina's house, near the center of town, where I slept like a baby in the hammock she offered. I made this portrait of her with a sieve that was found on the patio.

Graciela Iturbide
Serafina, Juchitán,
Oaxaca, Mexico, 1984

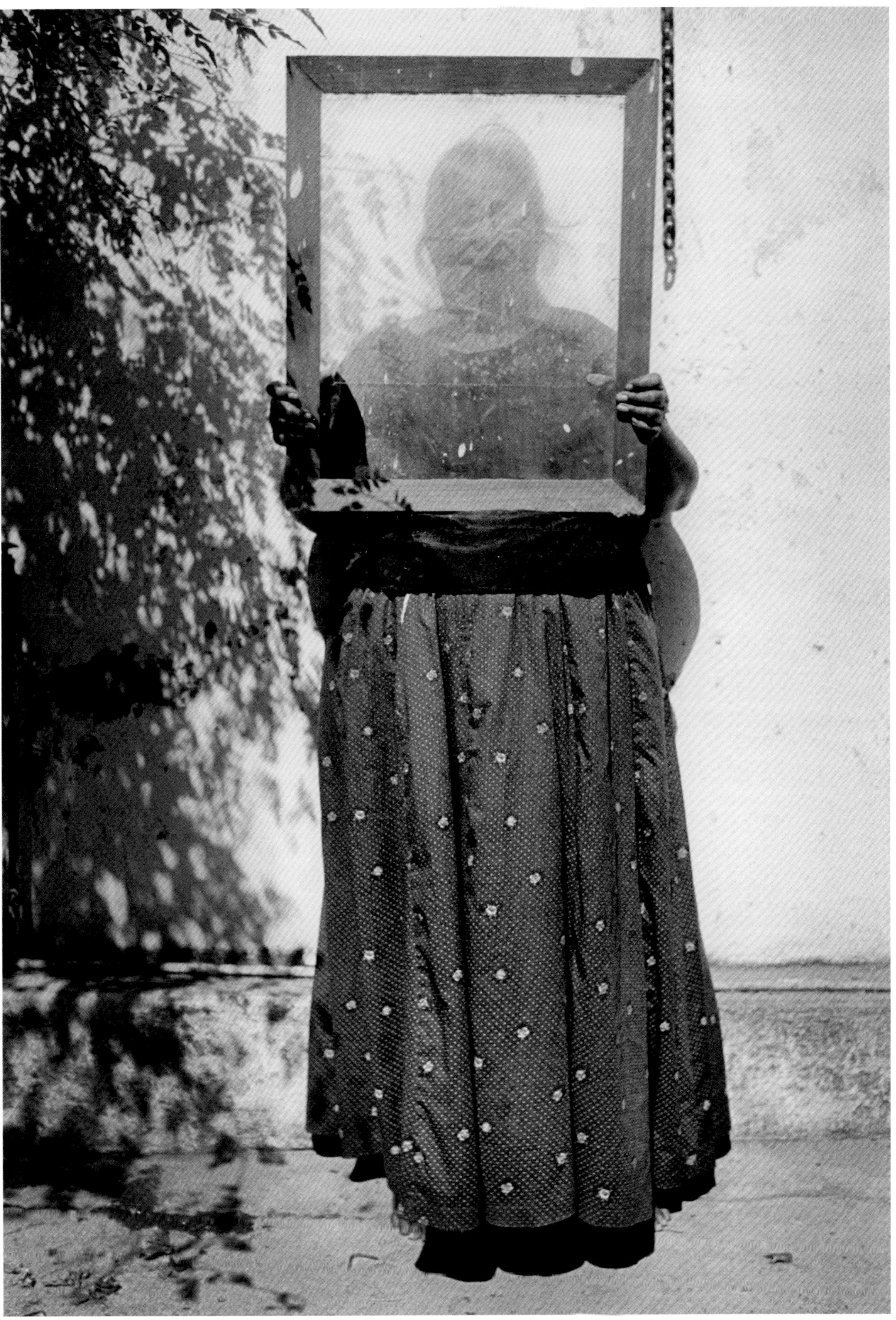

When I undertake a project, I never start with a preconceived idea. In Juchitán,
I began by going out walking with no fixed destination. That is how I came across
this girl combing her hair. I titled the portrait *La niña del peine* (Girl with hair-comb),
because Manuel Álvarez Bravo was very fond of a flamenco singer called La Niña
de los Peines. In this way, just walking around, I encountered many of the scenes
I portrayed in Oaxaca: a little boy sleeping, covered in a lace veil; a window with
slaughtered chickens in it, still dripping with blood; a circus artist with a monkey;
and household altars and shrines.

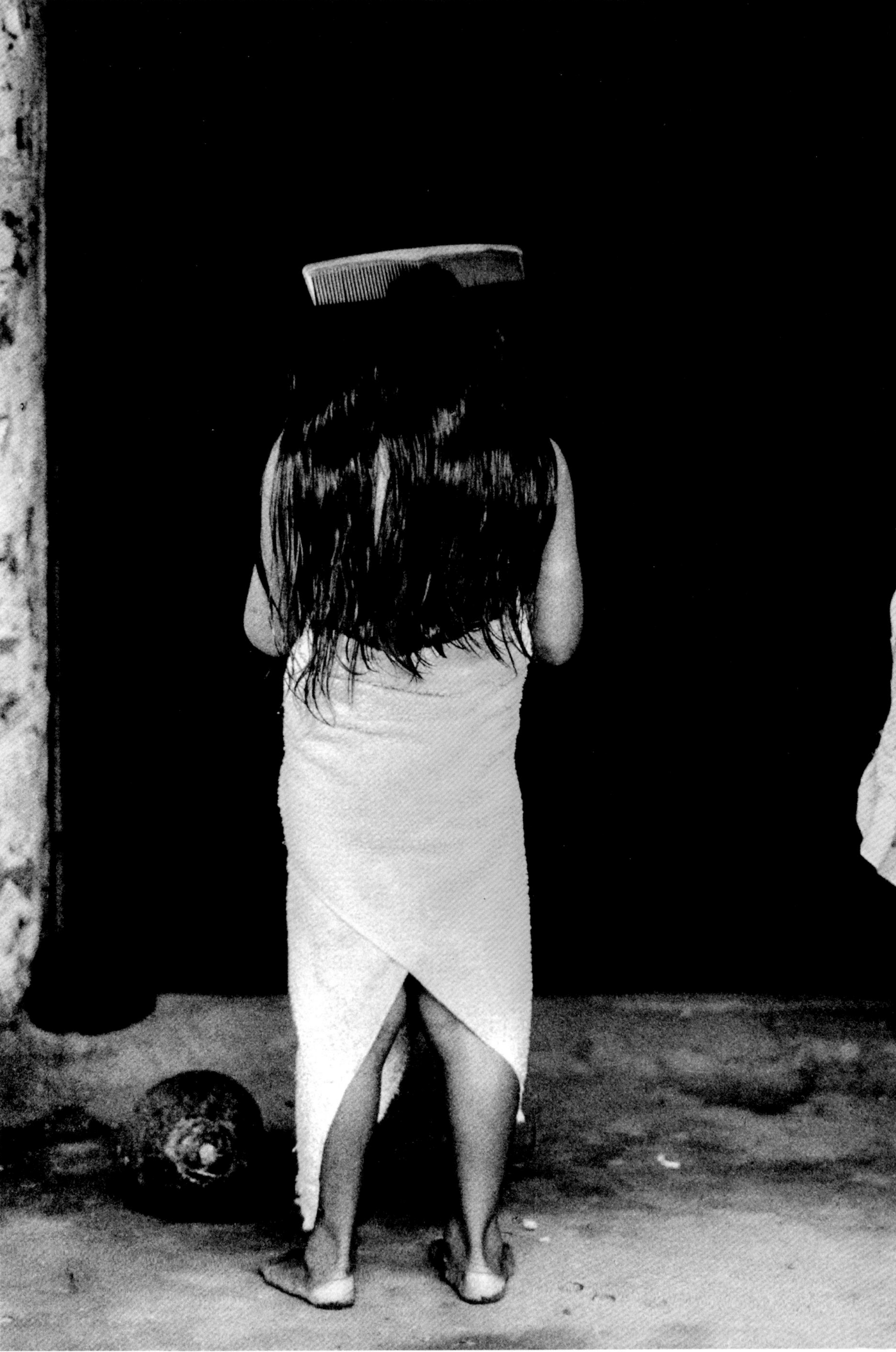

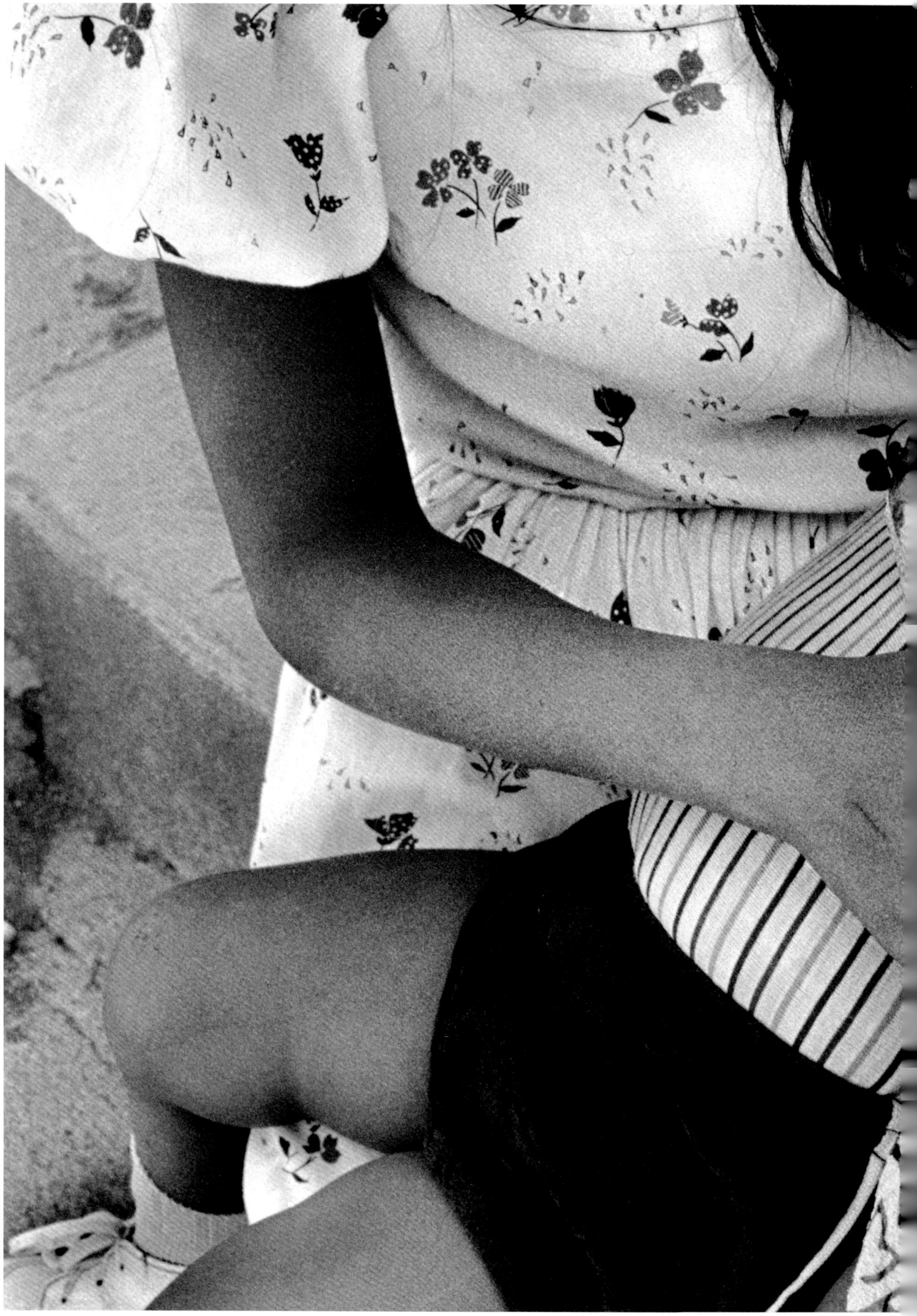

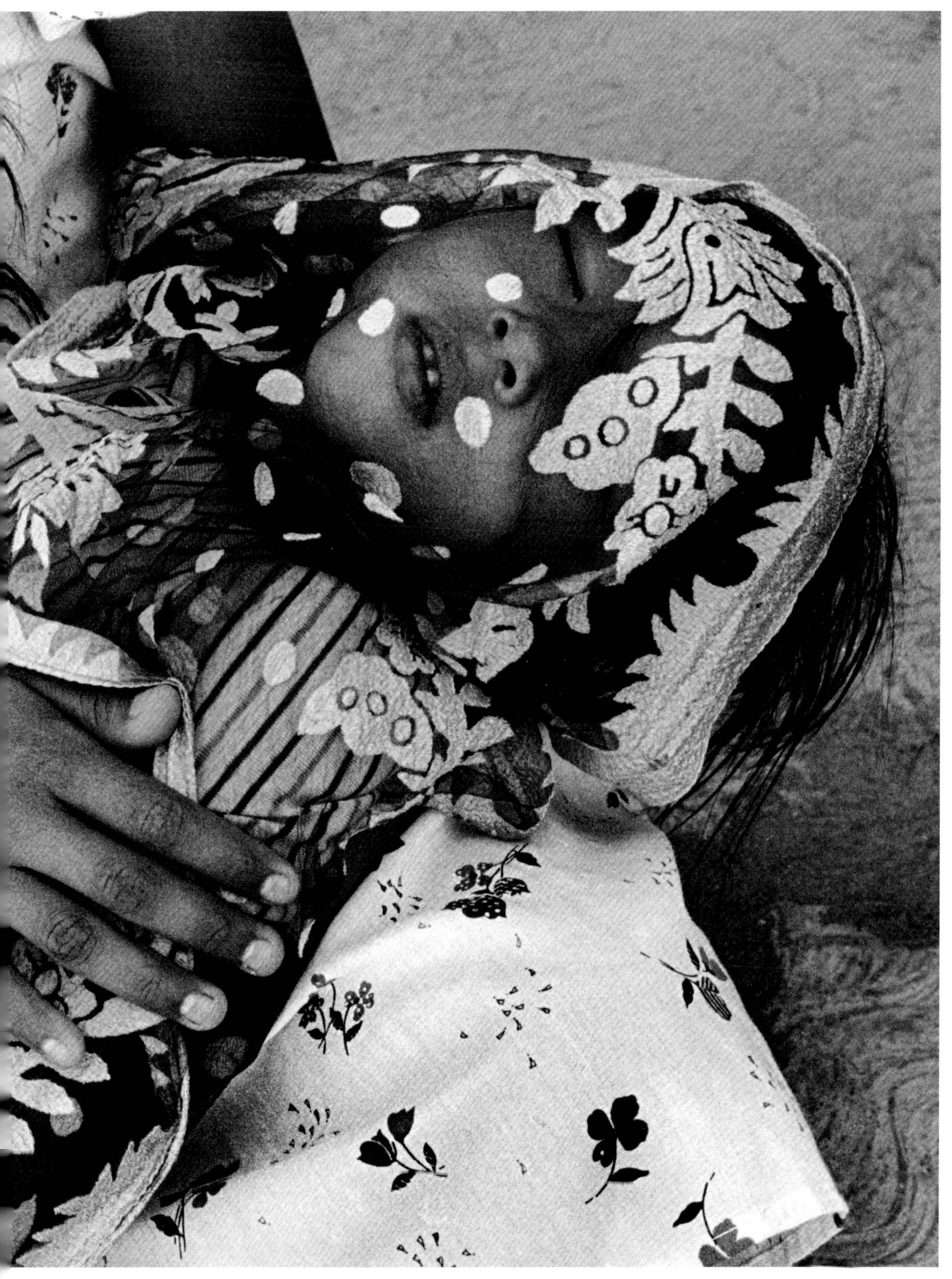

Like Serafina, most of the friends I made worked in the market. The bustle and animation of the market appealed to me from the beginning. Women of Juchitán go there to sell or barter; men cannot enter, though *muxes*, who are genderqueer, can. On one of my first visits, having just arrived in Juchitán, I encountered a woman carrying a cluster of iguanas on her head at one of the entrances. The iguanas had their mouths sewn shut so they wouldn't bite. She was about to take the iguanas off her head, when I said, "Please, please, señora, wait a moment." I took the photos without thinking much about it. I was lucky to have a dark background, but with enough light on the woman's face and the iguanas for them to stand out against it. Because of the low angle, the iguanas seem to form a headpiece or a crown. This photograph became my most famous and most often reproduced image; it has been used in murals, on book covers and posters, as clay figurines, and on labels for bottles of mezcal. Before she died, the iguana lady knew how well and widely her portrait was known.

Graciela Iturbide
Nuestra Señora de las Iguanas
(Our Lady of the Iguanas),
Juchitán, Oaxaca, Mexico, 1979

48

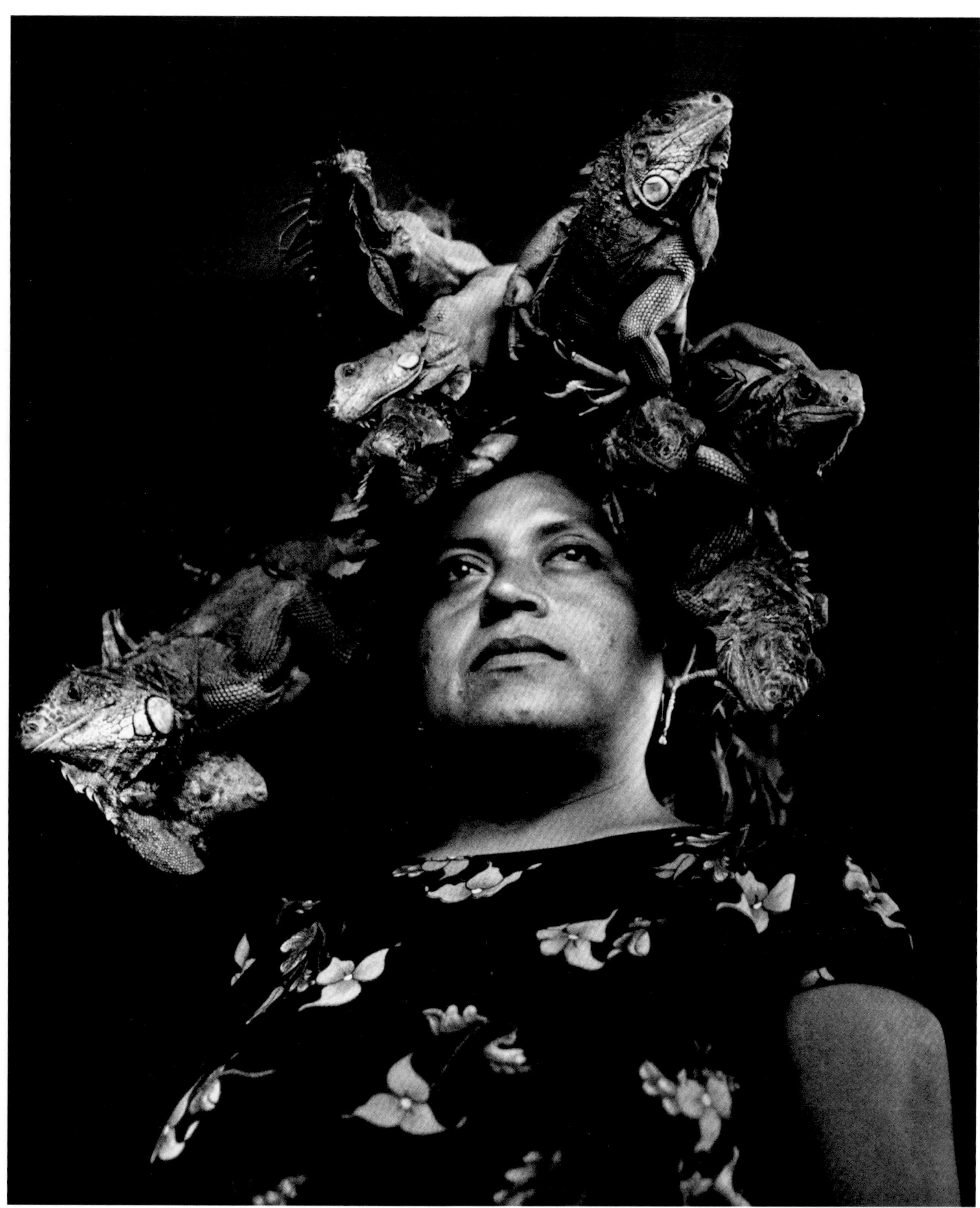

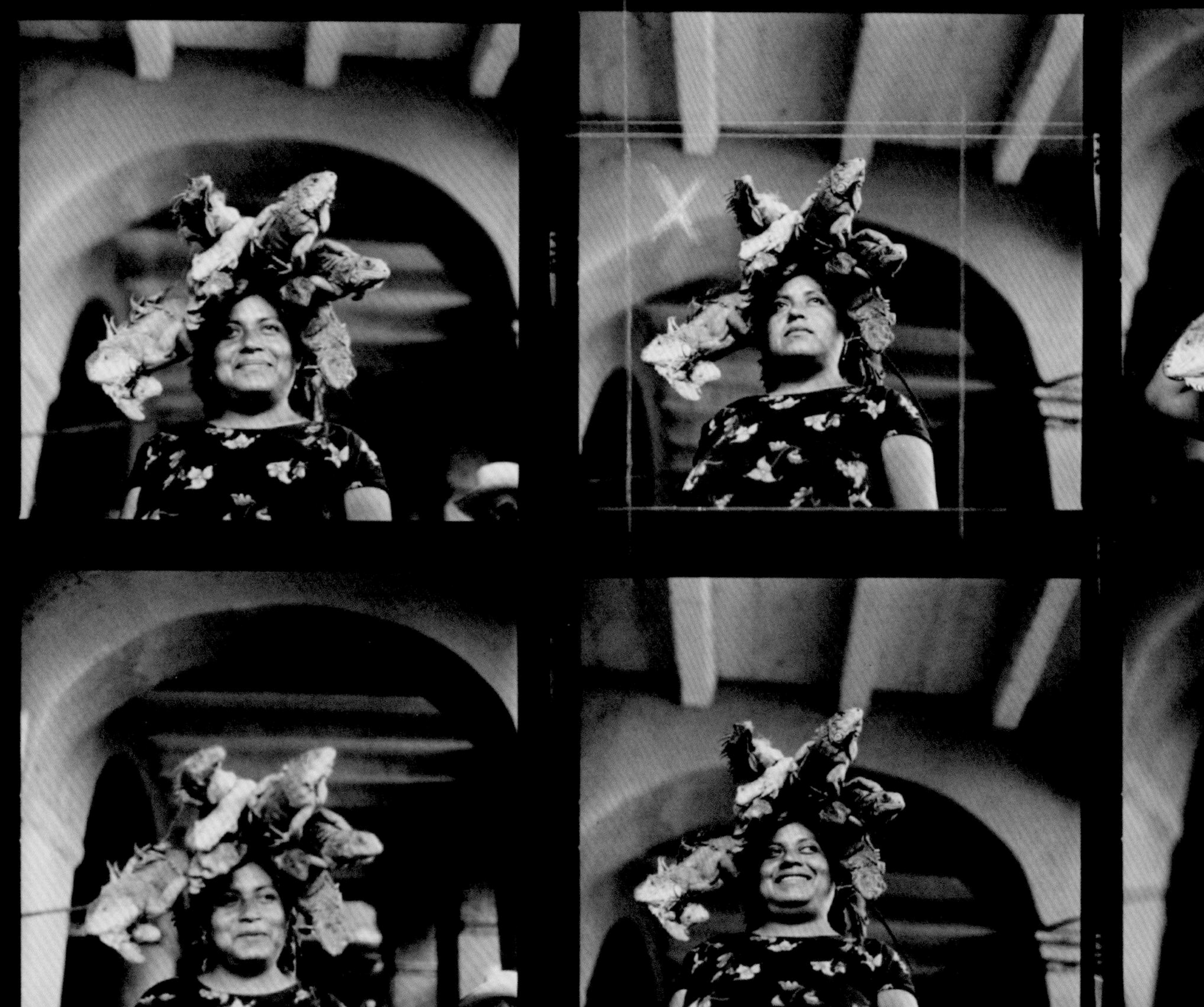

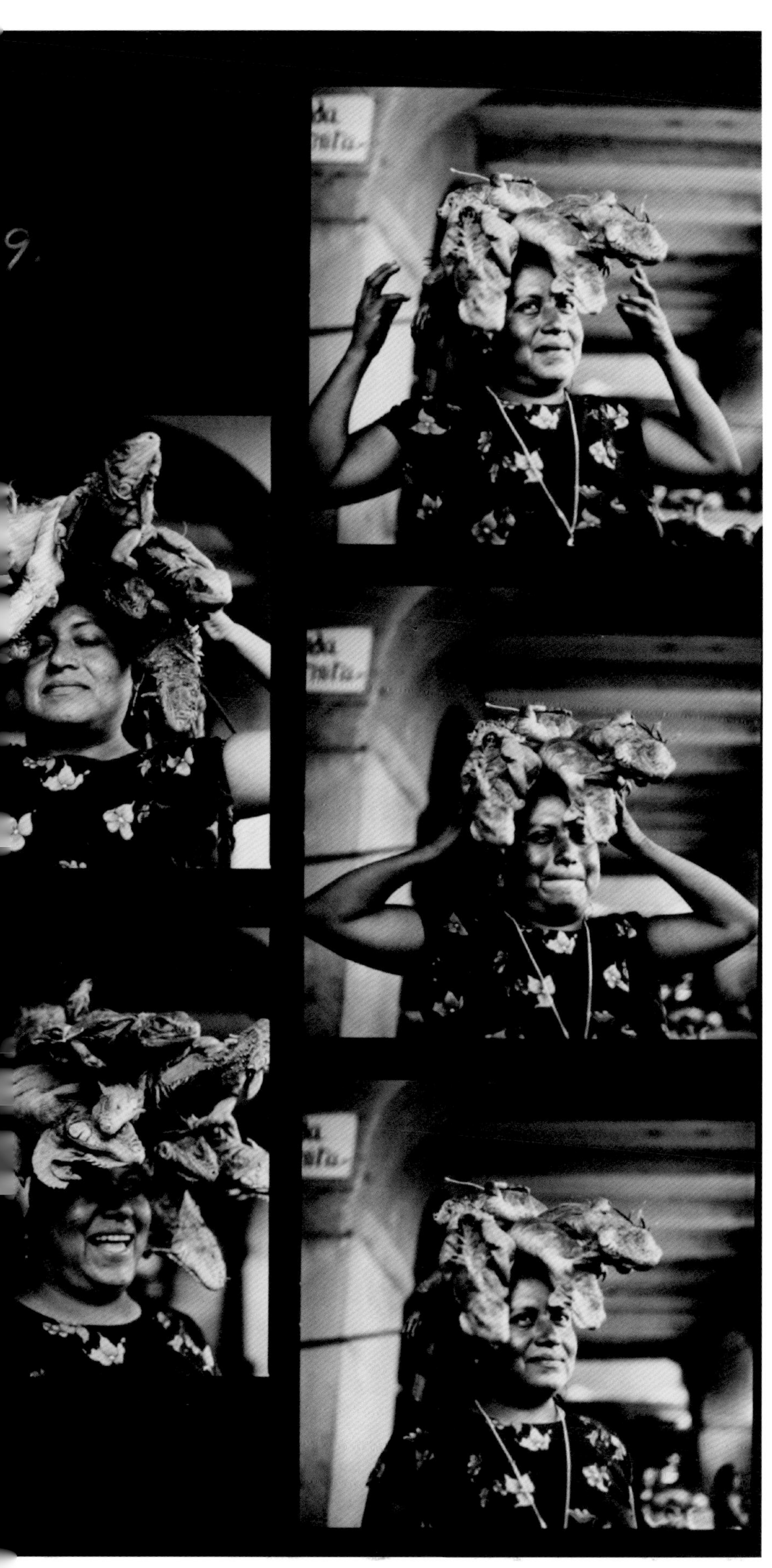

Graciela Iturbide
Contact sheet of *Nuestra Señora de las Iguanas* (Our Lady of the Iguanas), Juchitán, Oaxaca, Mexico, 1979

I was in a cantina having a drink and a snack with Macario Matus, my camera in plain view, when a *muxe* approached me. She was dressed in men's clothes at the time, and said, "Ay, my love, why don't you take a photo of me?" "Certainly," I replied. Her name was Magnolia. We went to a room in the upper part of the cantina, where she seemed to live—that's where she kept her women's clothes anyway. She changed several times, and I made photographs with the clothes and poses she wanted. I considered it my role to give her the confidence and freedom to express herself in front of the camera. This was my only encounter with Magnolia. I like the portrait where she is holding a mirror the best; it shows the identities of someone who is both masculine and feminine. When I received an award in Paris for my work in Juchitán, *Le Monde* published a full-page spread of one of the portraits I made of Magnolia. I left it as a present for her at the cantina.

Graciela Iturbide
Magnolia con espejo
(Magnolia with mirror),
Juchitán, Oaxaca, Mexico, 1986

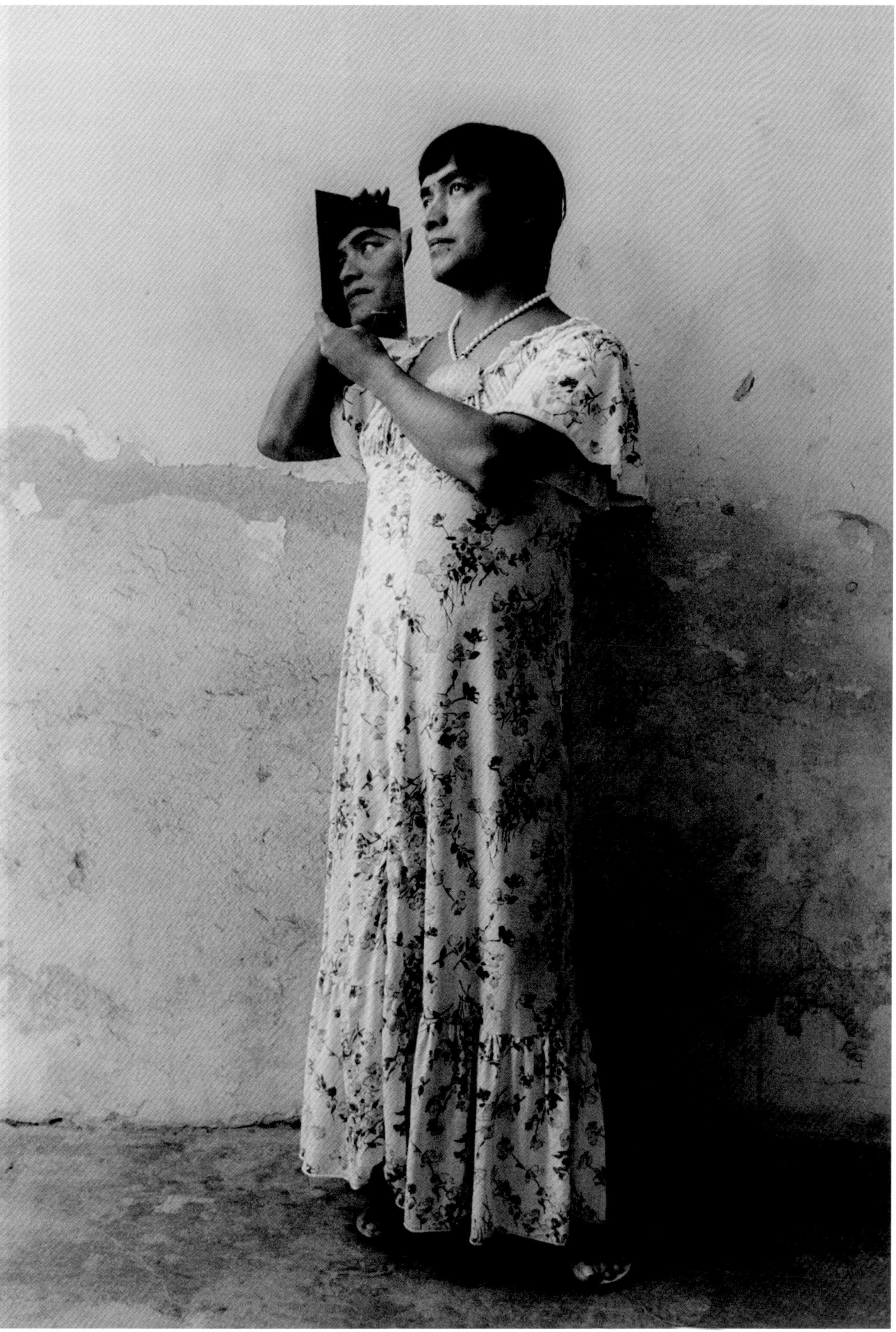

See What Happens

I took a portrait of Macario Matus's wife (she's the one whose hair is flying about) with a friend or cousin at Casa de la Cultura in Juchitán. There was a sheet of acrylic lying around, and it occurred to me that if I placed it in front of the women, the image would be slightly diffuse. A couple of young people from the COCEI held the sheet while I took the photo. When I developed the negatives, I discovered that their hands were visible. I loved the effect and left them in the image.

As you're photographing, your imagination ignites and leads you to use what is at hand. Everything is chance. At the time, I thought, "Let's see what happens if I use this."

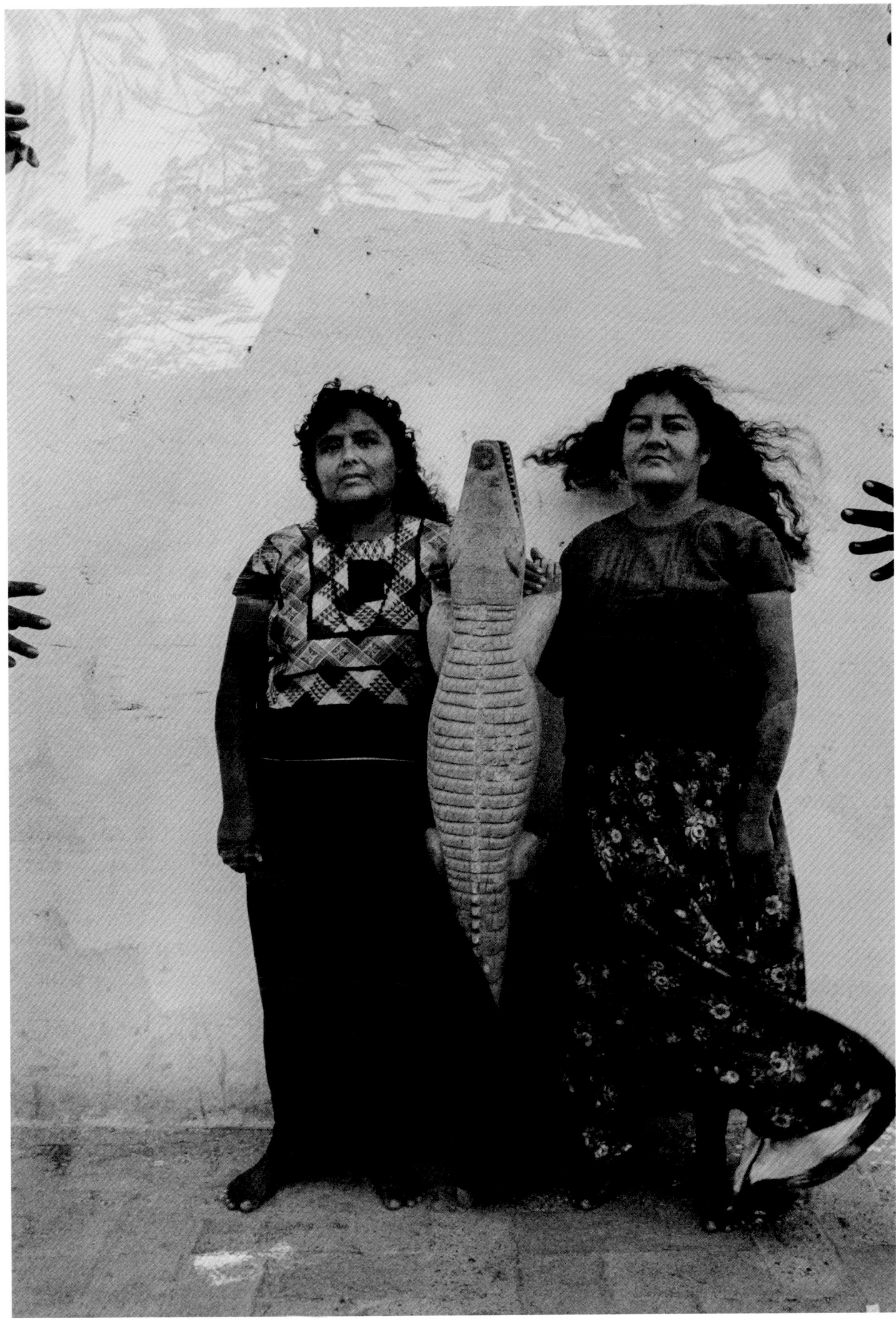

The graveyard in Juchitán has monuments that resemble small houses. When someone dies, their loved ones mourn for nine days. During that time, as a show of affection and respect, they place flowers on the grave.

One afternoon, I visited the graveyard and made a portrait of a woman who was gathering wood. There were birds in the sky, but I wanted even more, so I combined two negatives, one with the woman and the other with only the flitting birds. Just as I may use what is at hand, I may also see ways to add to a picture so it becomes what I envisioned after the photograph was taken.

Graciela Iturbide
Cementerio (Cemetery),
Juchitán, Oaxaca, Mexico, 1988

Pages 58–59
Graciela Iturbide
Manos poderosas
(Powerful hands), Juchitán,
Oaxaca, Mexico, 1986

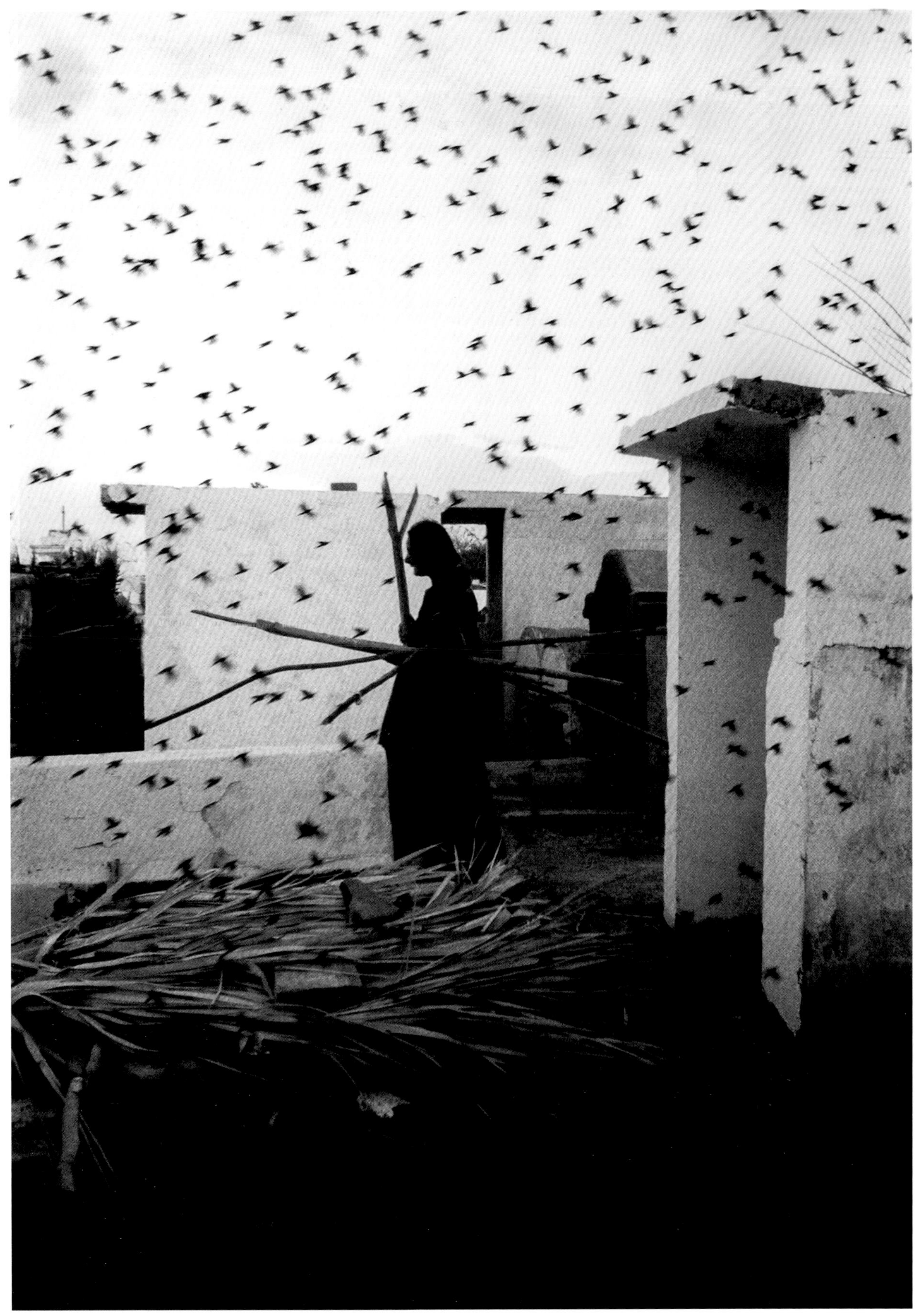

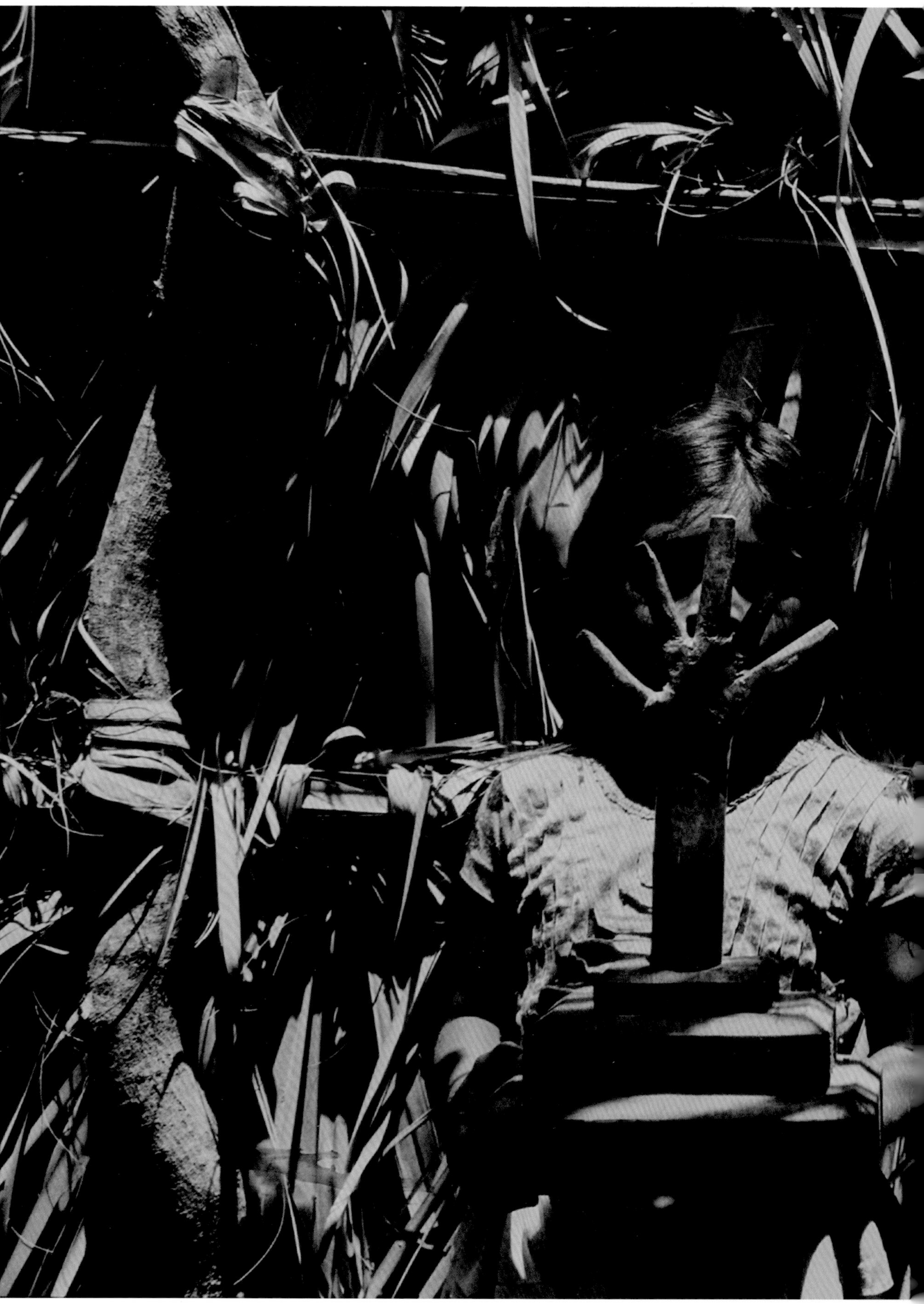

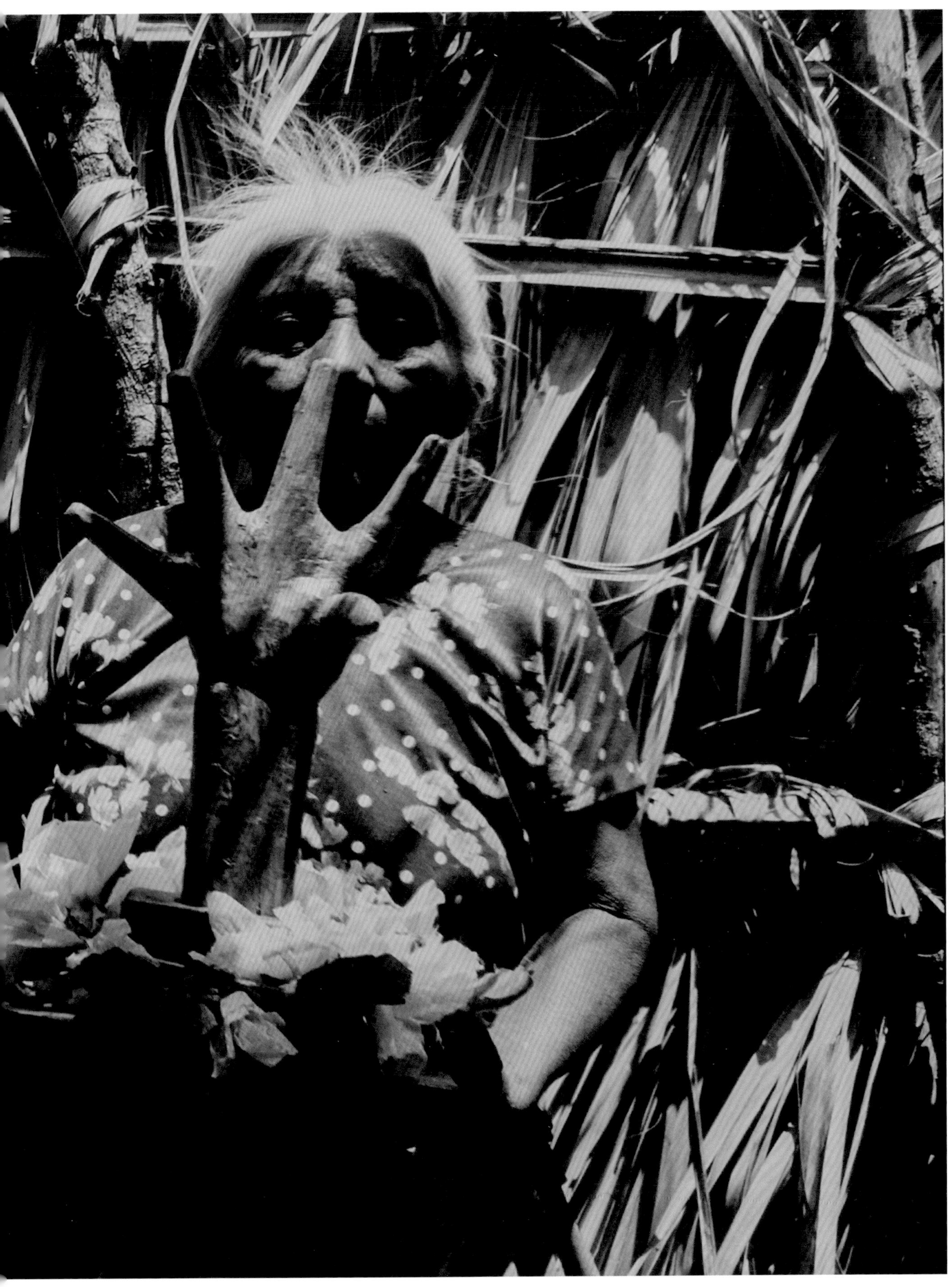

In Community

One day Leopoldo de Gyves, a friend who was one of the leaders of the COCEI, called: "Graciela, there are fireworks, there's an 'abduction' going on, you have to come!" The person being "abducted" was someone close to him, a sister-in-law or the daughter of one of his cousins, I can't remember. An abduction occurs when a young couple decide to run away together. The woman is "taken" to the man's family home, where they spend the night. The following day, all the women come to see if there is blood on the sheets, proof that the young woman was a virgin. The women inspect everything; they're really something else. Sometimes they bring chicken blood to simulate the loss of virginity. Lying in bed, the young woman is adorned with red tulips and confetti, and a kerchief for her head. Erotic songs are sung to her. The man's family takes garlands of flowers to the woman's family to formally annouce that she is no longer a virgin and is going to get married. These garlands, made by men, are received by women, who dance in a procession. The bride remains at the groom's home for eight days, resting until the marriage takes place, first in the presence of the couple's godparents, who give their blessing, and then in the church. Thanks to my friend in the community, I was able to photograph this tradition. I know of no other record of it.

Another lasting tradition in Juchitán is that of the "Holy Hands." The hands are found in the branches of a certain tree and then carved—very few people in the community have them. I like to describe them as "powerful hands," because it is said that people dream about them before finding them. They then take them home, make an altar, and adorn them with flowers. They respect them as they would a saint. I had heard about these hands before someone took me to see them. I was also able to see the little tree where they grow. Even Toledo was unaware of this tradition; he learned about it when I showed him my photographs.

Accepting Toledo's invitation to make an extended portrait of Juchitán provided me with an opportunity that changed the course of my career and started a lifelong friendship. I gave a selection of my photographs to Casa de la Cultura and published a book of the work, *Juchitán de las mujeres* (Women of Juchitán). The title came from Elena Poniatowska, who wrote the introduction. At first the title and her text seemed good to me, but I can now see how these choices exaggerated the dominant role of women in a way that wasn't present in my work. I recognized that while women had a stronger place in Juchitán culture than they do elsewhere—they handled the family finances, worked several jobs at the same time, drank, danced, and enjoyed themselves just like the men—they do not consider themselves matriarchs. Outside of Zapotec culture, Mexican women are resigned to a lesser role. While this contrast certainly interested me, I had no feminist agenda.

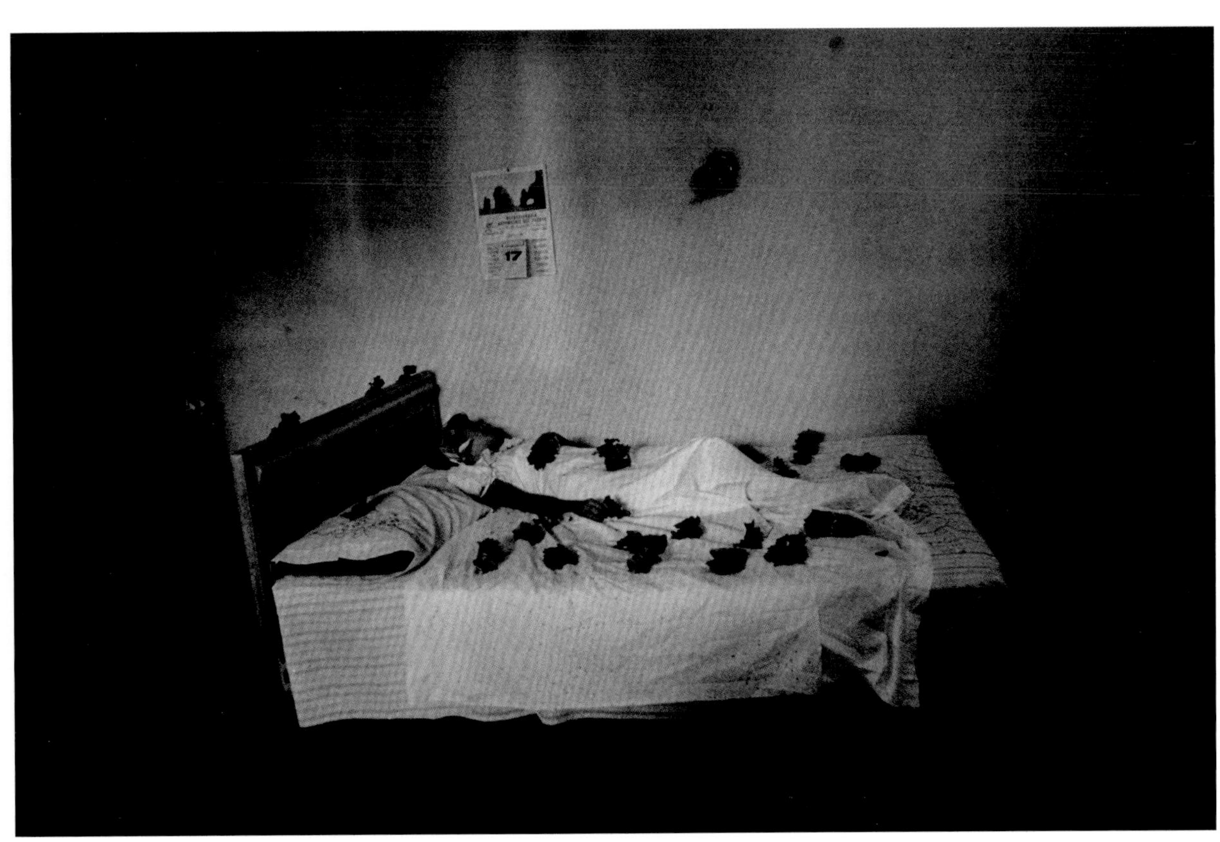

Above
Graciela Iturbide
El rapto (The abduction), Juchitán,
Oaxaca, Mexico, 1986

Pages 62–63
Graciela Iturbide
Mujer ángel (Angel woman),
Sonoran Desert, Mexico, 1979

61

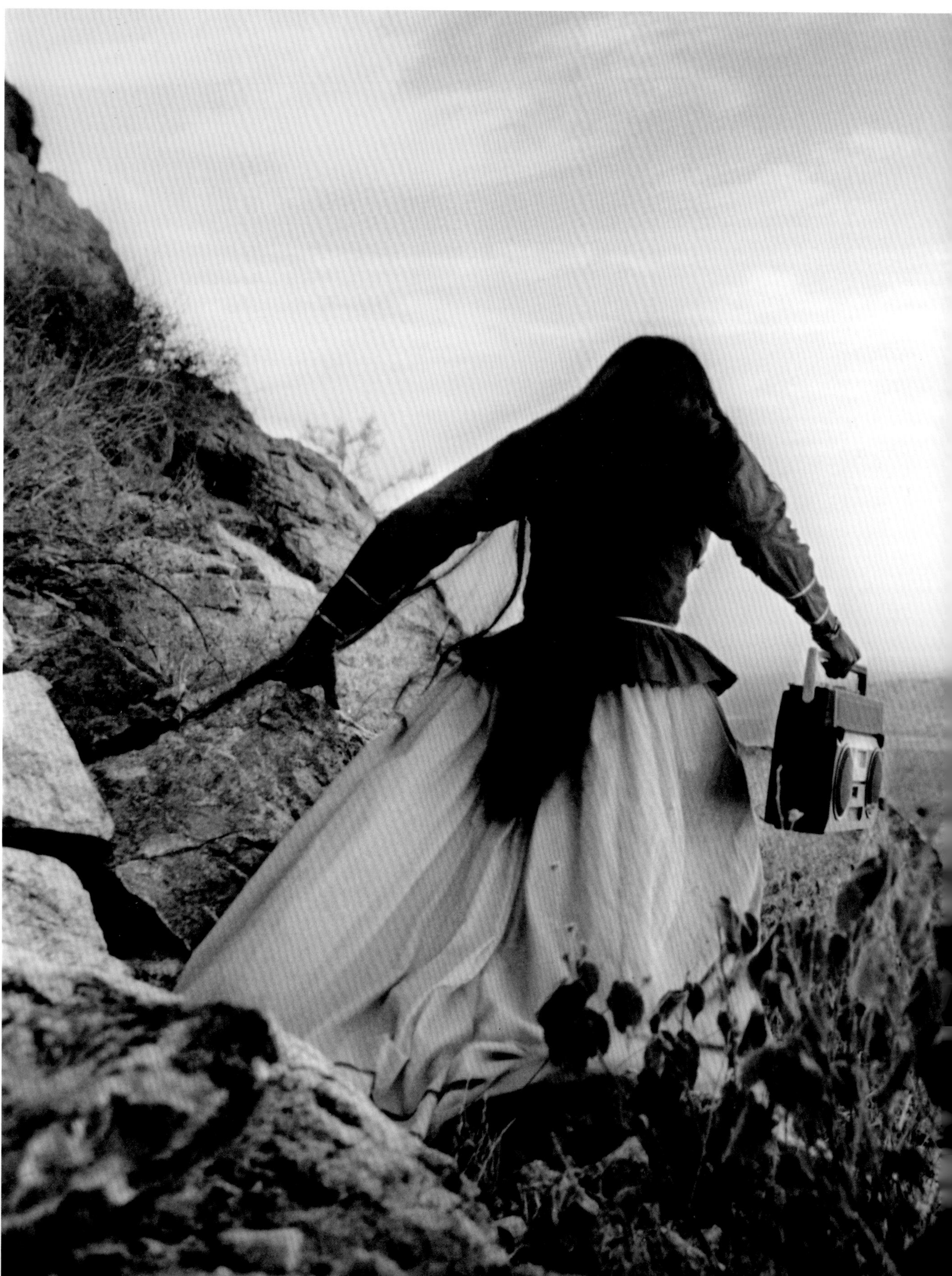

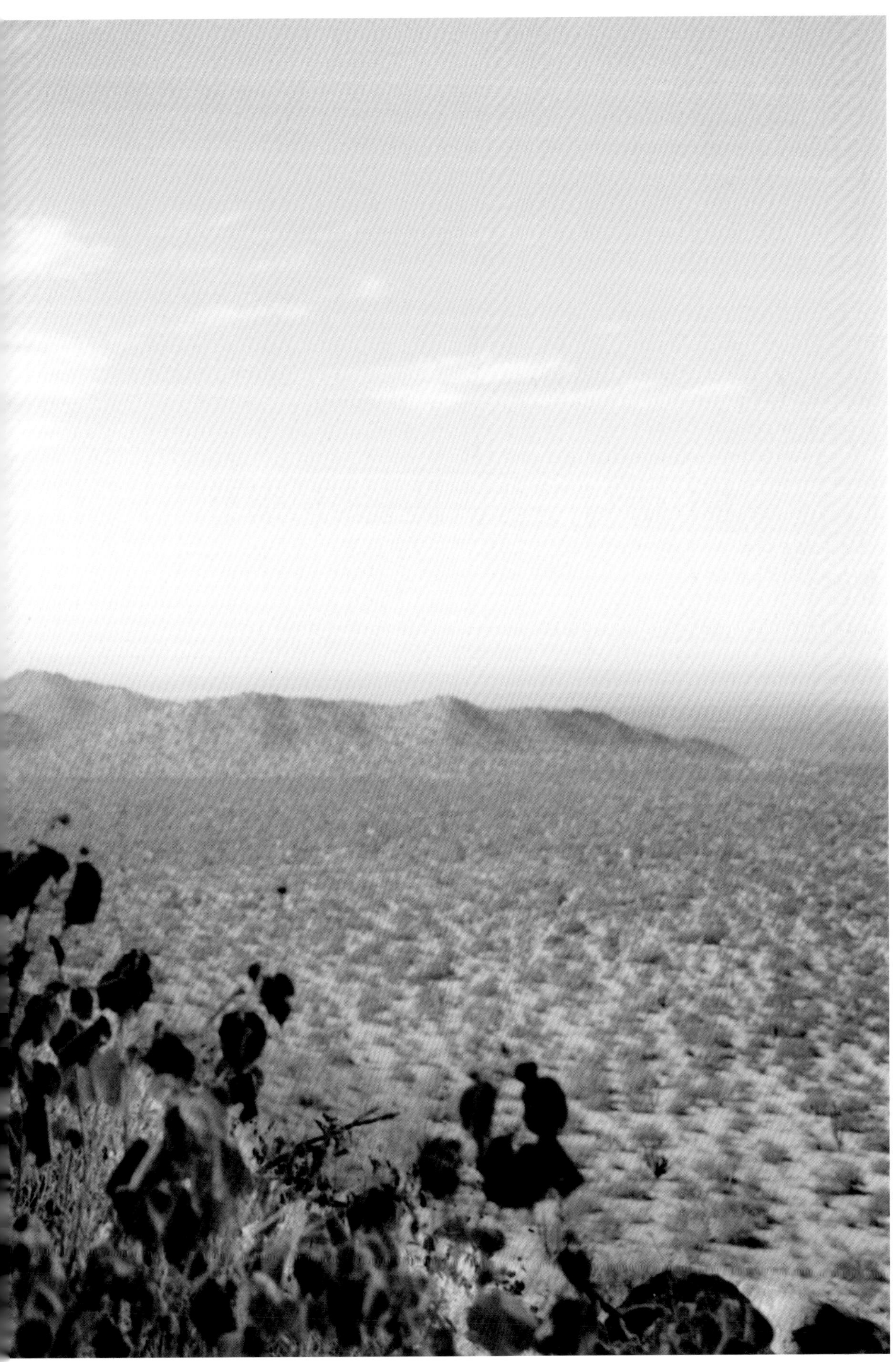

When I arrive in a new place, I follow my imagination, but I also try to speak to Elders and other locals to get to know their history and way of life. In this way, I don't choose subjects, they arise through a mutual understanding with people. In the case of the Seri people, they sung songs about their life and rituals.

It is very important to me that the communities and people I photograph are involved in the process. I don't steal images. When I arrive in a new place, I'm clear about what I'm doing there; people know that they are going to be photographed. I don't have a telephoto lens or a tripod or a flash. I've always worked with a handheld camera, because it allows me to get close to people—I am always aware of the space I am in. In some ways, with the camera, I am asking to take photos. If they don't give their consent, I don't photograph.

There were only five hundred Seris still living when I photographed them in the Sonoran Desert near Hermosillo. The Seris are former nomads and their daily life is austere. The men go fishing and make sculptures; the women gather seashells and make necklaces. I couldn't walk out into the streets and expect to document their lives in the same way I have in other places. I lived with them for a month, and we established a familiarity between us. I made portraits of almost all the families in their traditional attire. One day, they wanted to show me some cave paintings, and I went into the desert with them. That's when I photographed the angel woman carrying the boom box (pages 62–63).

For me, this photograph represents the transition from their traditional way of life and the way capitalism changed it. The Seris believe that money promotes inequalities and individualism—they did not want to become a divided society, so they traded their folk art for electronic equipment like radios. I liked the fact that they hadn't lost their traditions, but had taken what they needed from American culture. I don't pretend to make photographs that speak to the truth of what Mexico is all about, but I can feel the way culture is changing and try to capture what it's like to live through that.

I don't remember taking the photo. I was far along in the process of working on a book about the Seris when Pablo Ortiz Monasterio, who edited the book with me, discovered the picture in my contact sheets: he saw a woman with her boom box almost falling into infinity. I hadn't. This image is a gift that the desert gave to me.

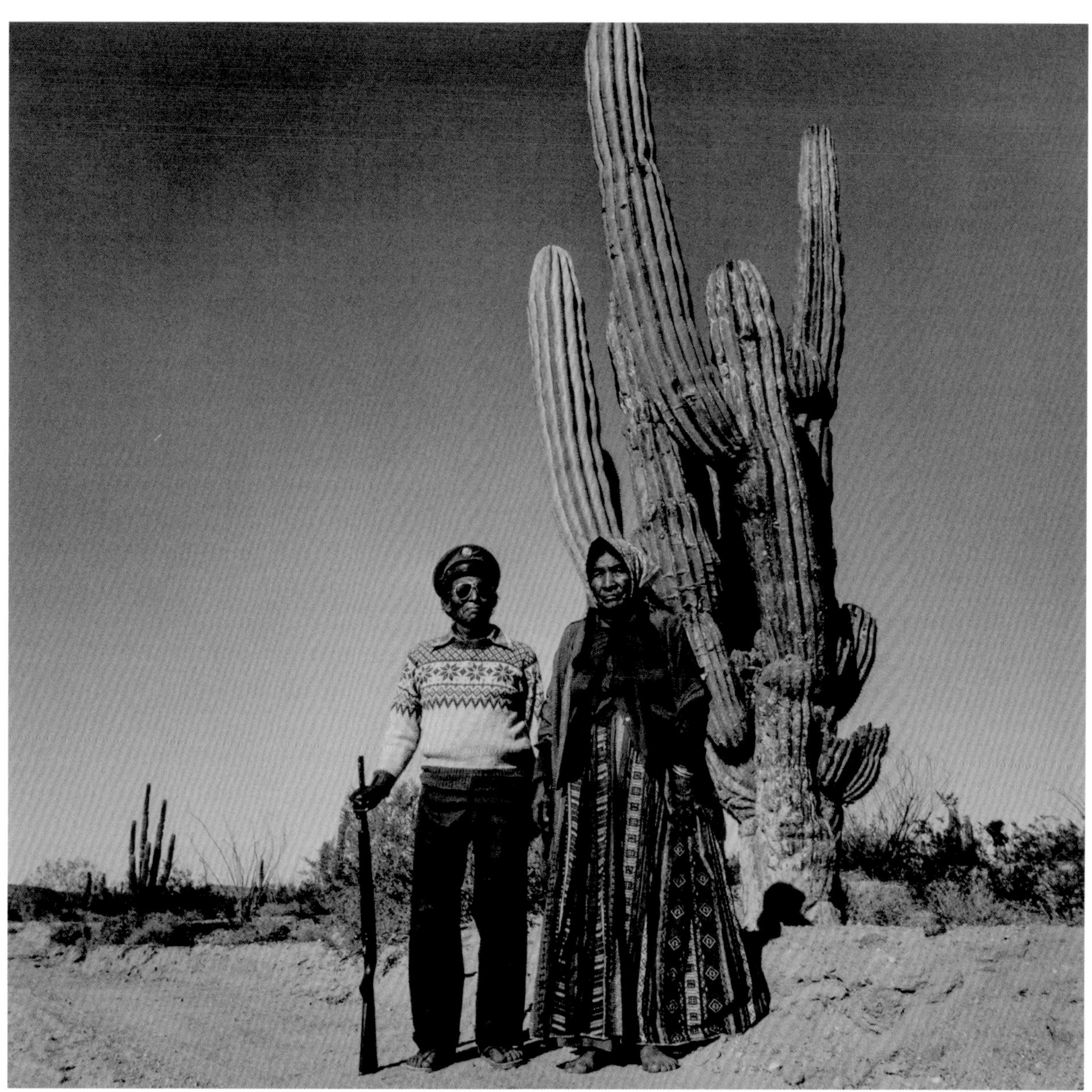

65

Mexicans are accustomed to living alongside death. There are many, many traditions and festivals centered on the theme. On feast days, people go to the cemetery; they take food, sing songs, maybe even take along a piano. On the Day of the Dead we give each other sugar skulls with our names on them to eat. We may play with death, but we also are afraid of it. This is why we try to face it straight on.

I first heard about the ritual slaughter of goats in Oaxaca's Mixteca region from the painter Sergio Hernández, who was then living in Paris. He was born in one of the villages where the practice takes place and shared with me his childhood memories of the bloody walls, ground, and rivers after a sacrifice. Some time later, I was able to see it with my own eyes. The goats travel long distances, grazing for several months until they are well fattened for the annual rite, which takes place in October and November. Dozens of people, including whole families, slaughter the goats—hundreds of them. They are skinned and butchered, and the meat, hide, viscera, horns, and hooves are used for food, shoes, buttons, and other objects. *Mole de caderas*, made from the hip joint, is a traditional and much-loved local dish.

Blood is everywhere. Only one goat is spared, wreathed in flowers, and led in a dance. In many of my images of the slaughter, life and death are conjoined. If the photograph of the white body of an unborn kid had been taken in color, the water would be visibly stained with blood.

Curator and writer Osvaldo Sánchez came with me to the goat slaughter so he could work on a text that would go with my pictures. But we each had very different experiences and impressions of it. I found myself immersed in an erotic and biblical world filled with the blood of sacrifice. Before killing the goats, the participants cross themselves to ask for forgiveness.

For Osvaldo, it was terrible; he could not continue watching and left (though he wrote an excellent text). I stayed and finished my work and ate mole. If I had gone without a camera, I'm sure my reaction would have been similar to Osvaldo's. There is a kind of trance that comes over me when I have the camera in my hands. When I'm taking pictures I even forget that I have a camera. I forget about everything. Light comes, death comes, people go in and out—it's like theater.

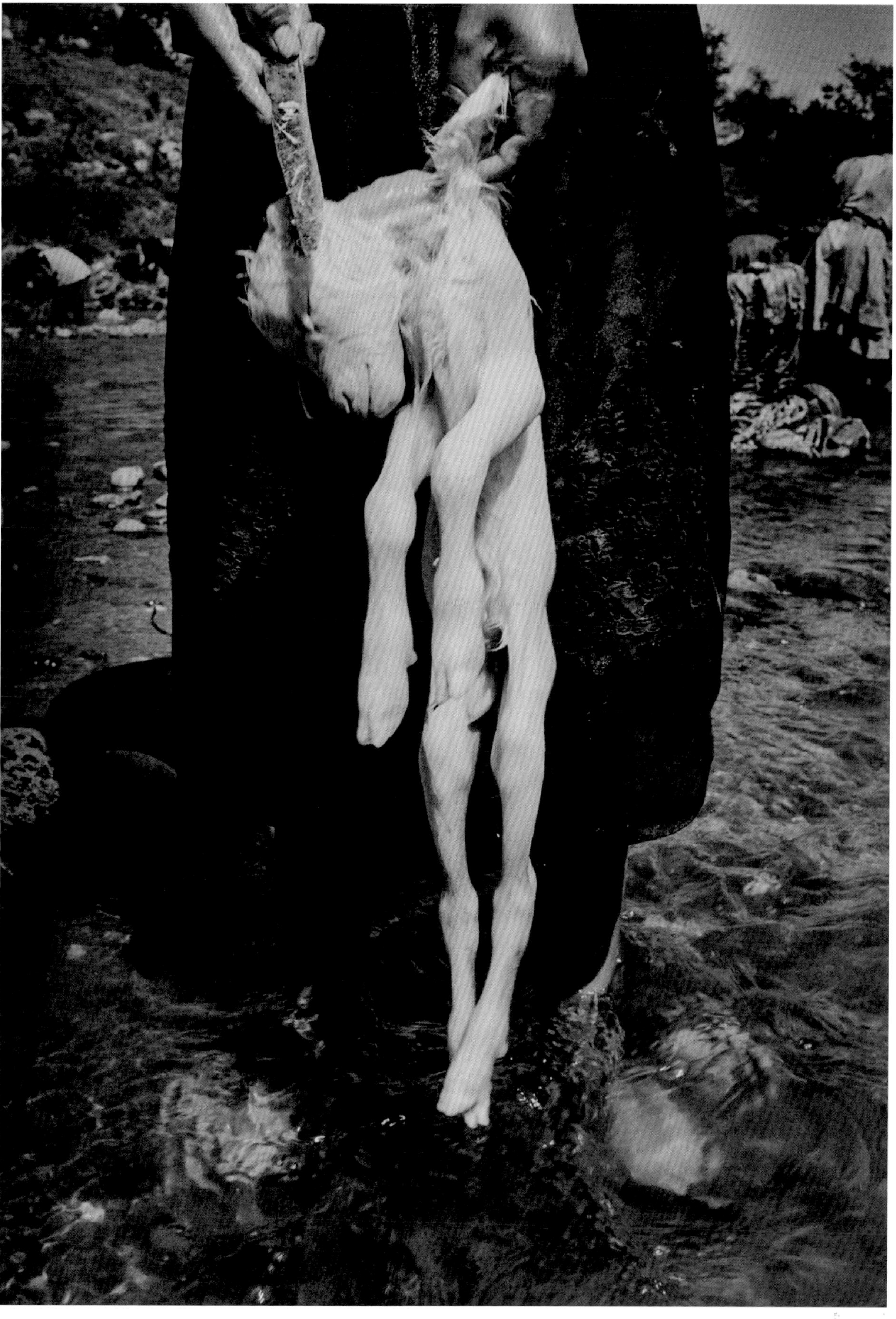

With My Eyes Shut

When I lost my daughter Claudia, I became obsessed with photographing death, especially children dressed as *angelitos* (little angels) after they die, as is the custom in Mexico. I felt the need to involve myself in the deaths of others, perhaps in order to come to terms with my own pain. In rural Mexico, I came across some people carrying an *angelito* to the cemetery. I asked permission to take photographs. They agreed—the whole family even posed—and they opened the coffin so I could photograph the *angelito*. They allowed me to follow them to the cemetery in Dolores Hidalgo. On the way, the father turned to me with a startled, terrified expression. In the middle of the road was a body—half man, half skeleton. It was still wearing trousers and shoes, but had been pecked all over by vultures. It was as if Death were saying to me, "You want to photograph me? Here I am."

That is how I began photographing birds. Death appeared, and I thought, "That's enough! Don't keep living your suffering this way." In the cemetery, vultures were flying overhead, and I photographed the sky full of birds instead. All of this is to say that in life, everything is connected: your imagination helps you process reality. I lost my child when I was still relatively new to photography, so photographing has been a sort of therapy for me. What you experience in life is connected to what you dream about and what you dream to what you do, which ends up in your pictures.

Graciela Iturbide
Cementerio (Cemetery),
Coahuila, Mexico, 1987

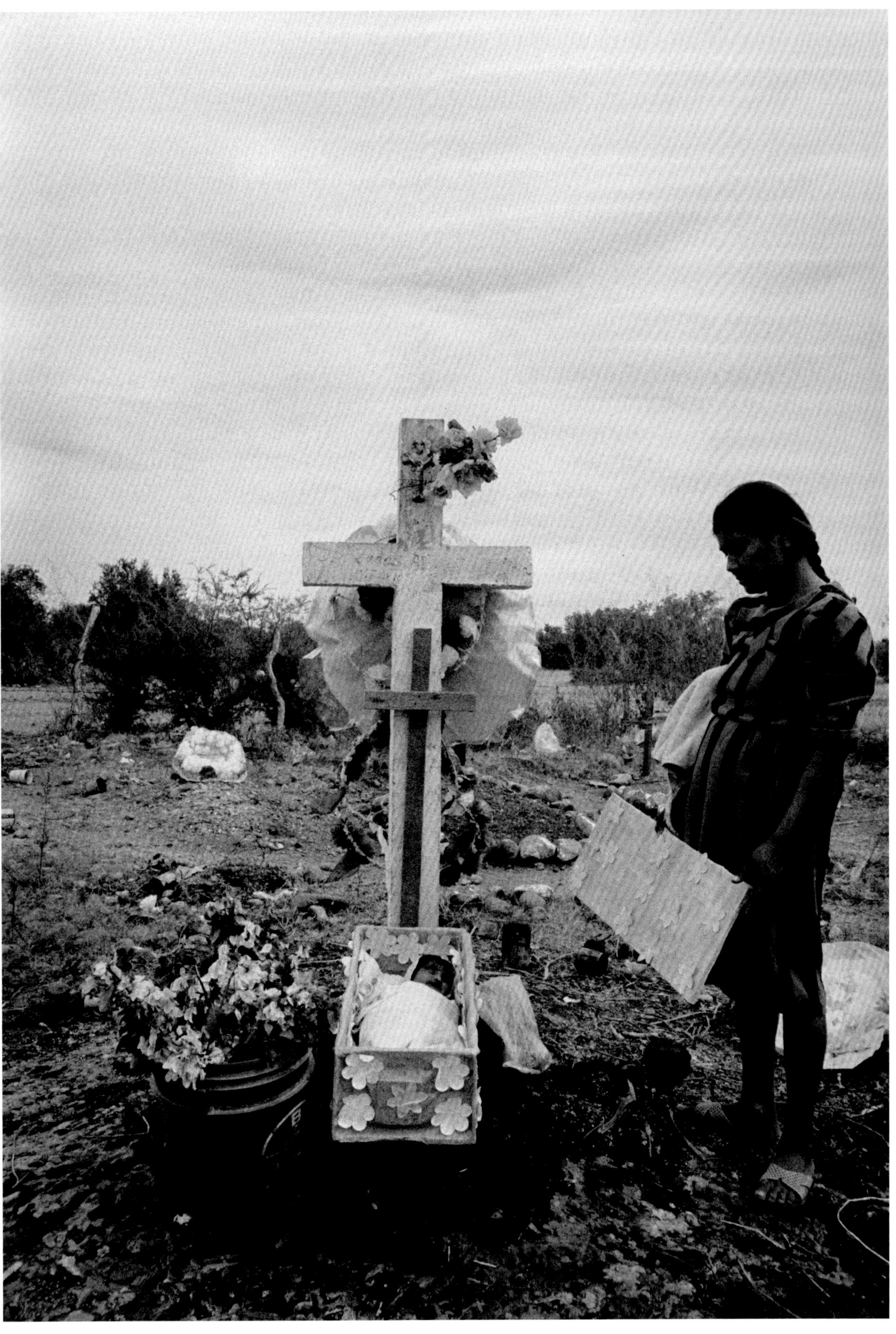

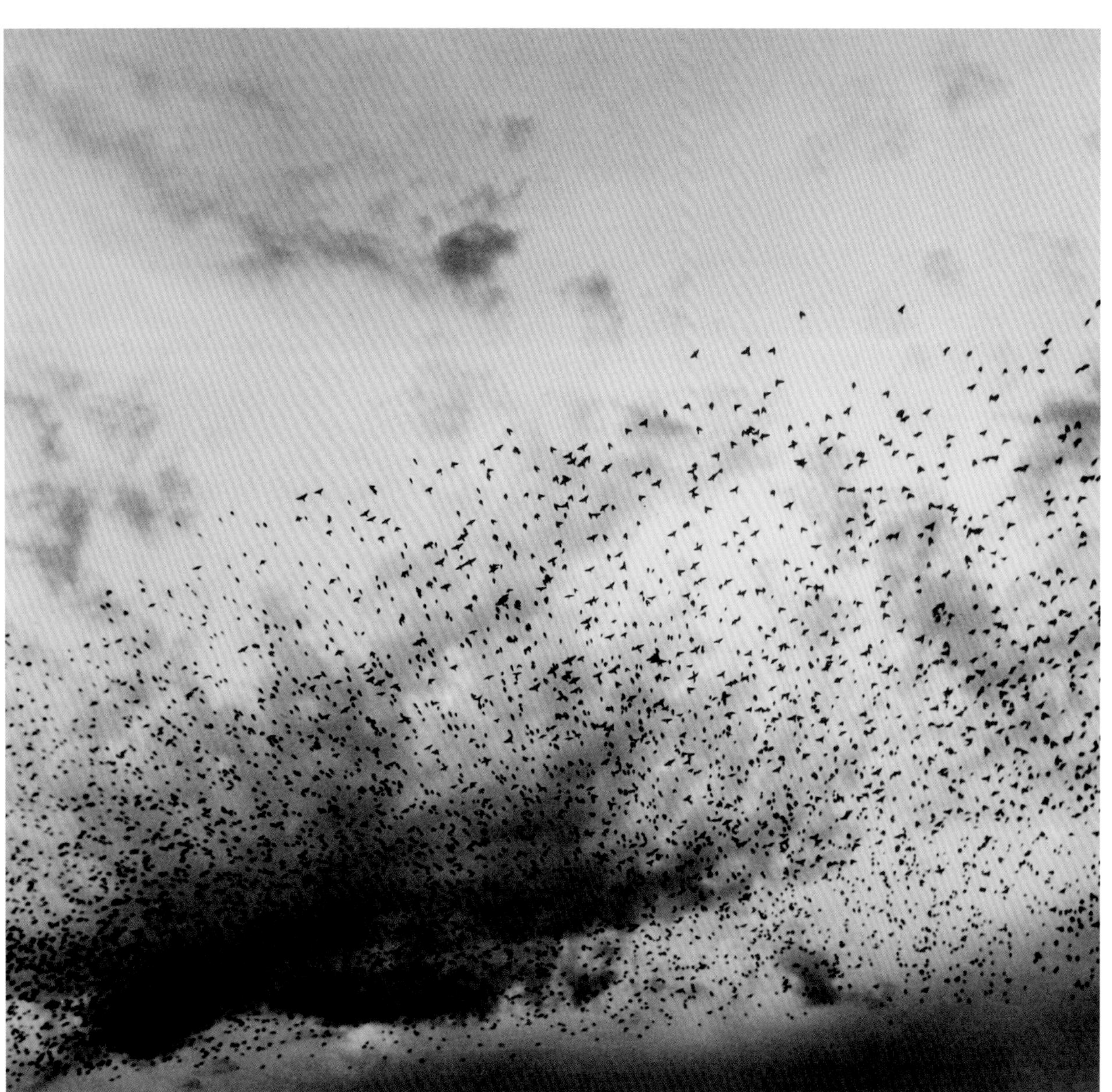

Graciela Iturbide
Pájaros (Birds), Dolores Hidalgo,
Guanajuato, Mexico, 1978

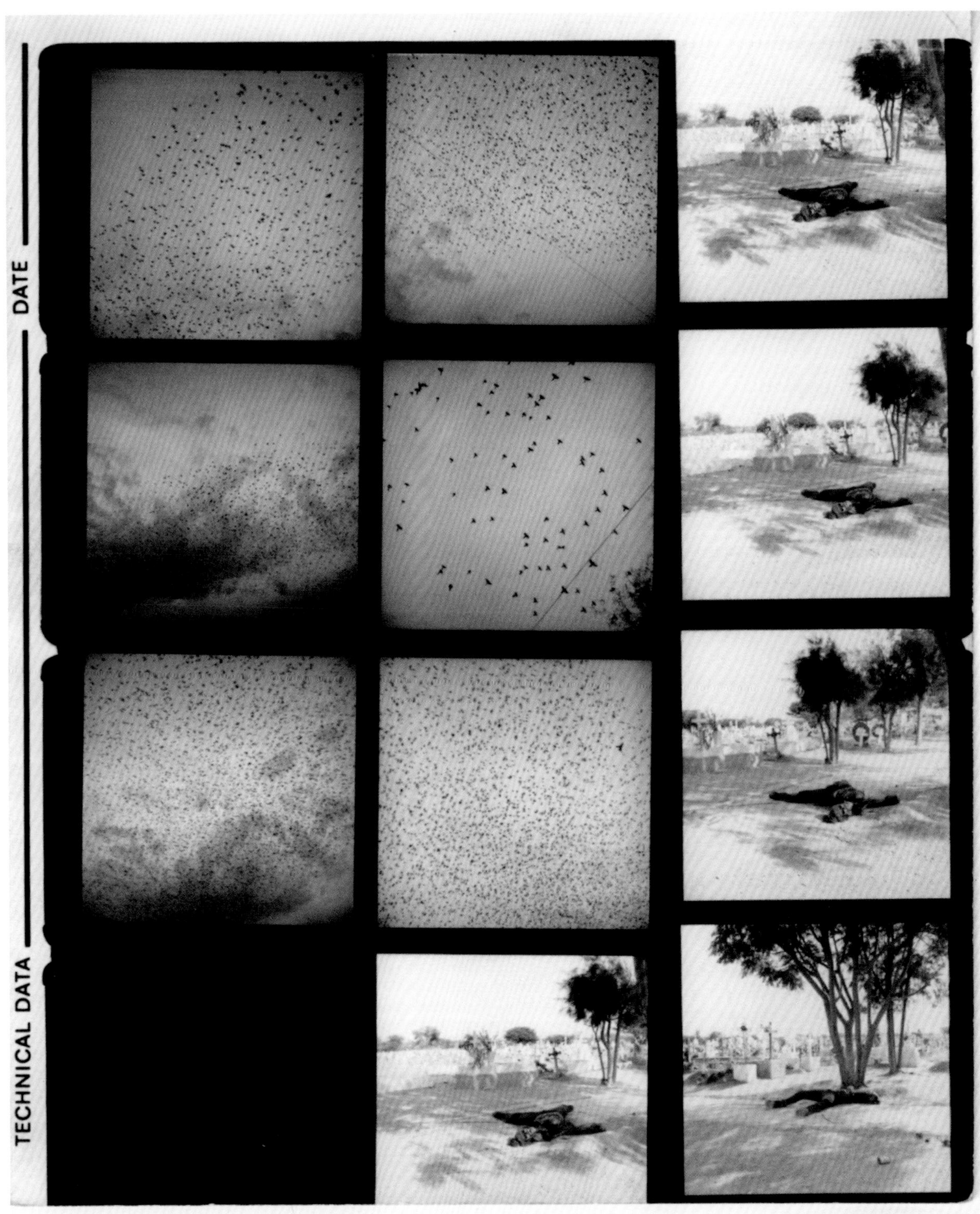

Graciela Iturbide
Contact sheet, Dolores Hidalgo,
Guanajuato, Mexico, 1978

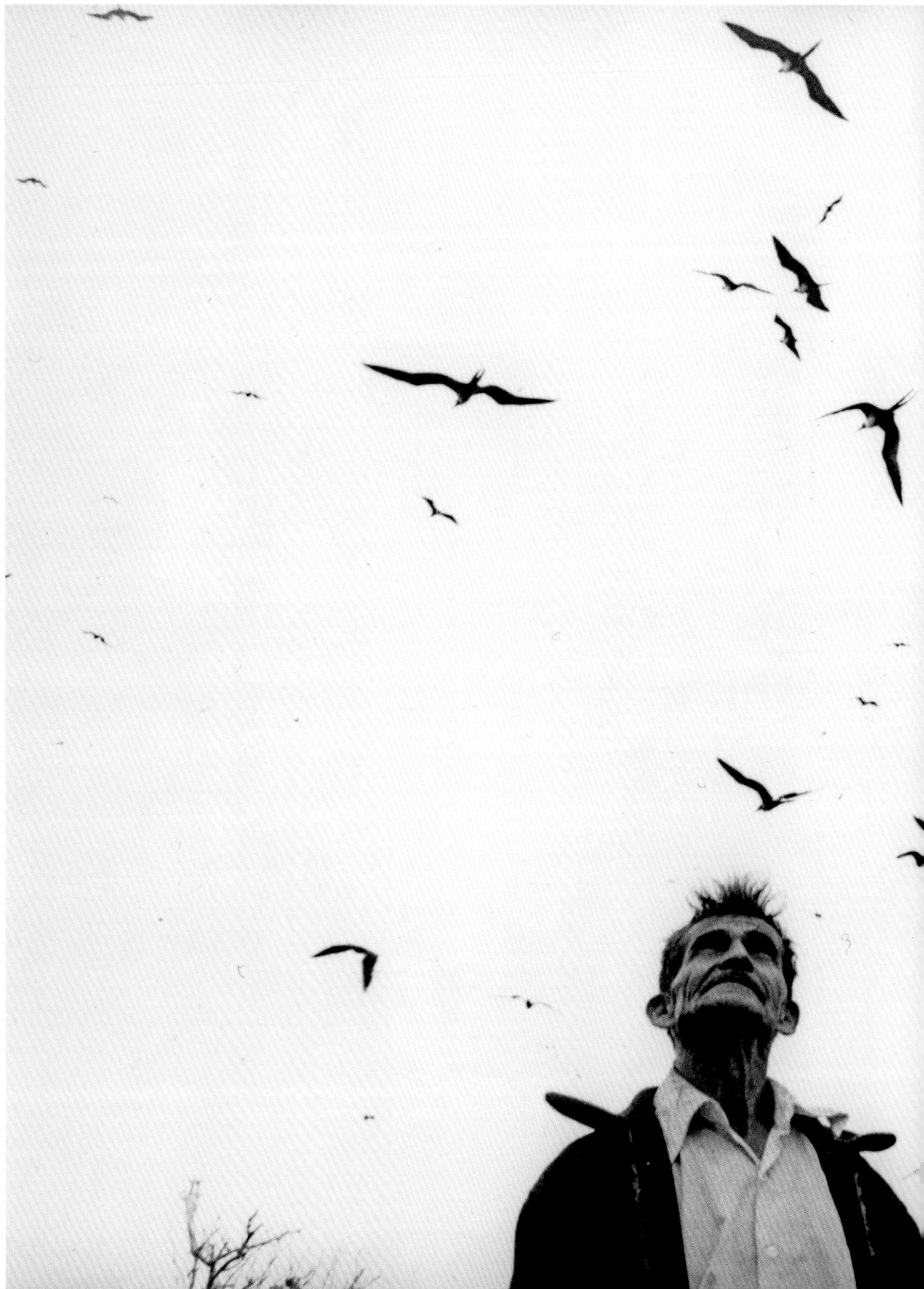

I can see with my eyes open and also with my eyes shut.

What happens in my dreams is as important to me as what happens during my
waking hours. I believe we all move between these two intertwined dimensions.
There is a quote from Brassaï that I like a lot; it has become a kind of motto for me:
"Life, therefore, cannot be grasped either by realism or by naturalism, but only
through dreams, symbols, and storytelling."

I make a habit of writing down my dreams as soon as I wake up, when they
are still fresh. Of course, they are no longer the same as when I was dreaming,
but something surreal remains.

One night in 1980, I dreamed of a man digging in the ground with a shovel
and repeating the phrase, "On my land, I will sow birds." Flocks of birds poured
out from where he dug. Four years later, in Nayarit, on the west coast of Mexico,
I came across a similar scene on Bird Island, a nature reserve with restricted access.
I was traveling with the artist Rowena Morales, and some fishermen agreed to
take us there—we stayed on the island for a couple of days, sleeping in a cabin.
We got to know the caretaker, who seemed the island's only inhabitant. I took his
portrait while hundreds of birds swooped above him (pages 72–73). The caretaker
himself appeared to be a bird. The relationship between my dream and the solitary
guardian of Bird Island was obvious to me when I saw the image in my contact
sheets. The lord of the birds went from dream to reality and from reality to photographic image.

Pages 72–73
Graciela Iturbide
El señor de los pájaros
(Lord of the birds),
Nayarit, Mexico, 1984

Right
Graciela Iturbide
Novia Muerte (Death Bride),
Chalma, Mexico, 1990

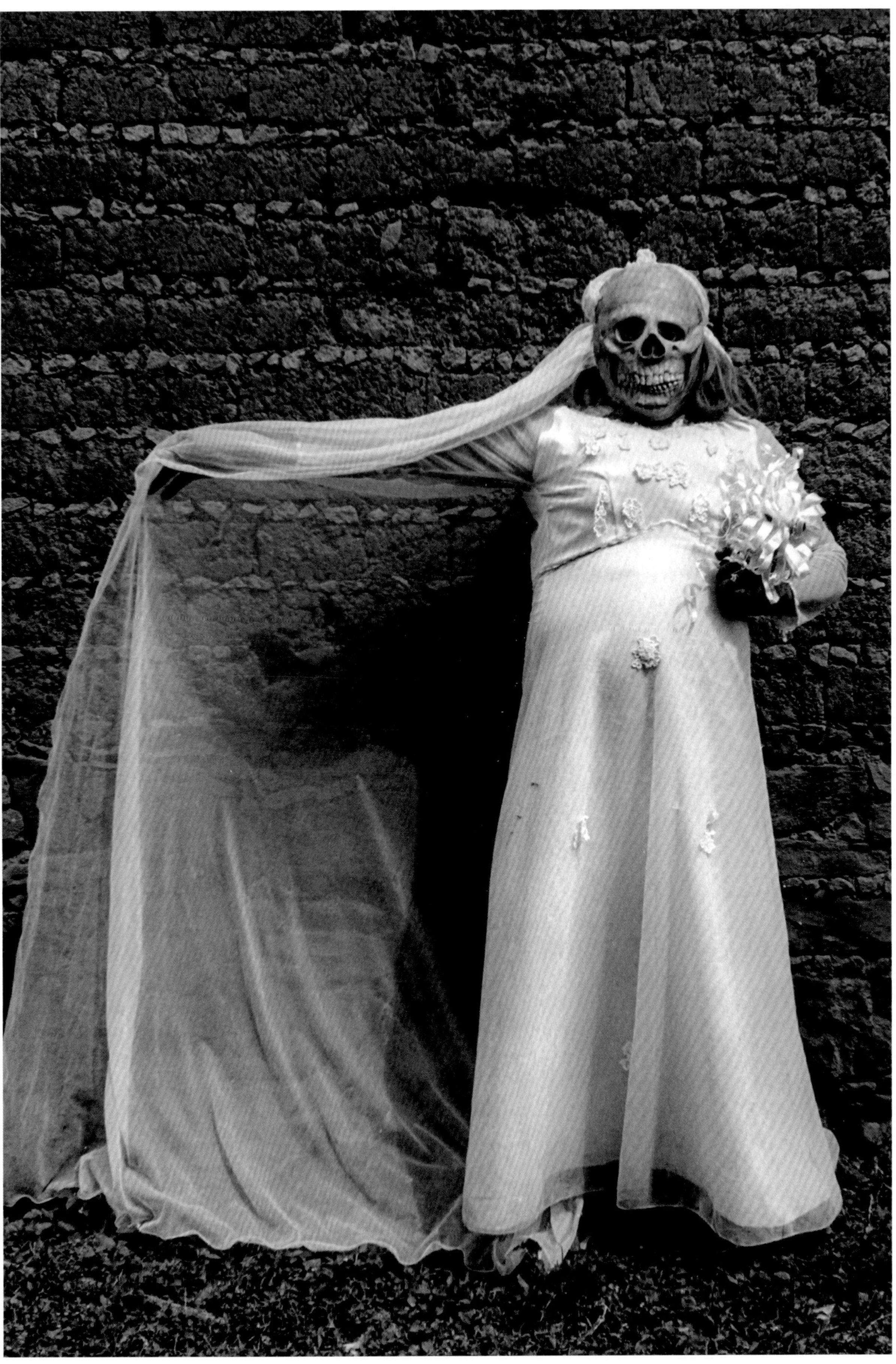

The Solitary Bird

I do not see animals with the eyes of a naturalist or an anthropologist, I simply record the places they occupy in our world and the ways in which we share a destiny.

I have always been fond of animals. There were dogs, cats, chickens, turkeys, parrots, toads, chameleons, chinchillas, and even water snakes around my childhood home. There were cages of canaries all over the place, cared for by my mother. When I was married, I had a Siamese cat who gave birth at the same time as me—both early under a rare moon. Pedro Diego Alvarado once gave me an iguana from Guerrero, named Brigitte. She died after spending a few months in my small apartment. Today I have a French bulldog named Hor—short for Horroroso—just like Manuel Álvarez Bravo's English bulldog.

But as a photographer, I have never actively focused on animals—birds, perhaps, have been my only deliberate pursuit. For the most part, the many animals that appear in my images have accumulated by chance. I have photographed them during travels and outings, within the context of daily life in cities and towns, as well as in the houses where I have lived. Over time, I realized they are a constant presence in my photographs.

I love to go to markets where animals are bought and sold for food, companionship, or religious ceremonies. I am struck by the relationships that people establish with animals, those they care for as part of their heritage or their family, and how they may also mistreat or neglect them, sometimes cruelly. This complexity can be seen in the representations of animals in my archive. Only cockroaches and rats disgust me, although I have images of rats from a temple in Rajasthan in northern India, where they are domesticated and considered sacred. Pilgrims feed them milk and fruit and sleep next to them. If a Hindu kills one of these rats, they must return with a silver one in its place.

Through my photographs, I have been able to recognize the symbolic value of animals, to see them as mythical beings. I have been influenced by Indigenous traditions and tales that speak of animals as *nahuales* or *tonas*—protective spirits, embodiments of souls, companions of the dead on their journey to the underworld. I have yet to photograph this custom that may or may not still exist in Juchitán: When a baby is about to be born, until the birth takes place, friends and relatives draw animals on the ground and then erase them before moving on to the next. The animal that is present when the baby is born is the baby's *nahual*.

Some time ago, at my home in Coyoacán, a bird came to visit me over the course of two or three months, pecking on my window. One of my first photos, taken when I was still an assistant to Álvarez Bravo, was of a tree full of birds. Perhaps my *nahual* is a bird.

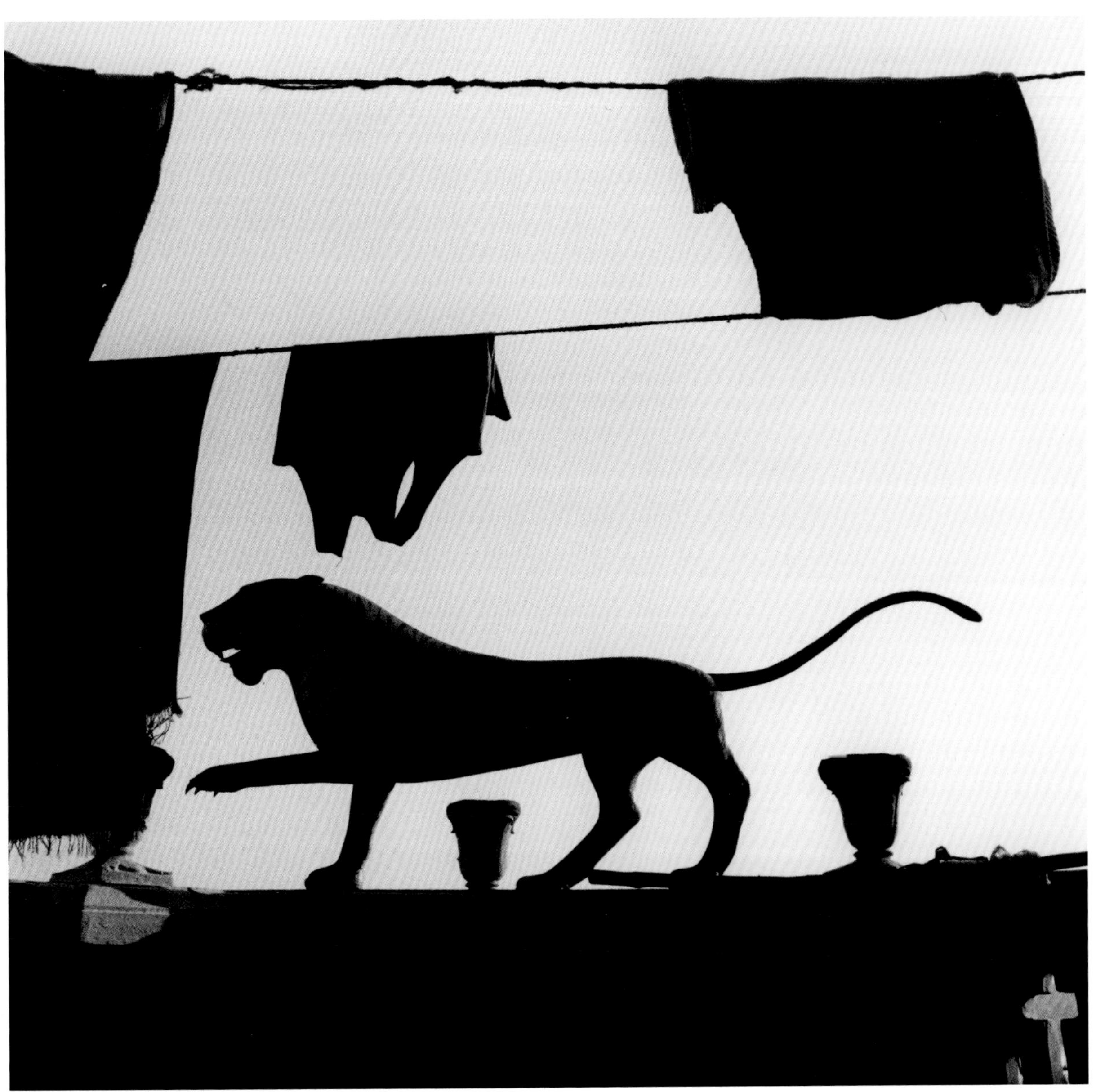

Graciela Iturbide
Untitled, Varanasi, India, 2000

Literature has helped me to understand the significance of animals in my own work.
I've learned the qualities of the solitary bird from *The Sayings of Love and Light* by
mystic poet St. John of the Cross by heart and have adopted it as my own:

> The traits of the solitary bird are five: first, it seeks the highest place; second, it
> withstands no company; third, it holds its beak in the air; fourth, it has no definite
> color; fifth, it sings sweetly. These traits must be possessed by the contemplative
> soul. It must rise above passing things, paying no more heed to them than if they
> did not exist. It must likewise be so fond of silence and solitude that it does not
> tolerate the company of another creature. It must hold its beak in the air of the
> Holy Spirit, responding to his inspirations, that by so doing it may become worthy
> of his company. It must have no definite color, desiring to do nothing definite
> other than the will of God. It must sing sweetly in the contemplation and love of
> its Bridegroom.
>
> **—St. John of the Cross, from *The Sayings of Love and Light***
> **(translation by K. Kavanaugh and O. Rodríguez)**

"The Conference of the Birds" by the Persian poet Farid ud-Din Attar was also a
revelation to me. The poem tells the story of a journey undertaken by the birds of
the world to search for the mythical Simurgh bird, who they wish to be their sover-
eign. Initially eager to set out, they are overcome by fears, each one giving a different
excuse for not going: the nightingale because it does not wish to be separated from
the rose, the falcon because it considers itself close to royalty, the goldfinch because
it is cowardly, and so on. Finally, with the guidance of a hoopoe, the wisest bird,
they work up their courage. The odyssey takes them across seven valleys: quest, love,
mystical knowledge, detachment, unity, wonderment, and annihilation. Only thirty
birds complete the trip. Upon arriving at the mountain of the Simurgh, they find
only a mirror, reflecting their own images. Jorge Luis Borges, a writer I greatly admire,
recounts the outcome this way in *The Book of Imaginary Beings*:

> Many of the pilgrims desert; the journey takes its toll among the rest. Thirty, made
> pure by their sufferings, reach the great peak of the Simurgh. At last they behold
> him; they realize that they are the Simurgh and that the Simurgh is each of them
> and all of them.
>
> **—Jorge Luis Borges, from "The Simurgh"**
> **(translation by Norman Thomas di Giovanni)**

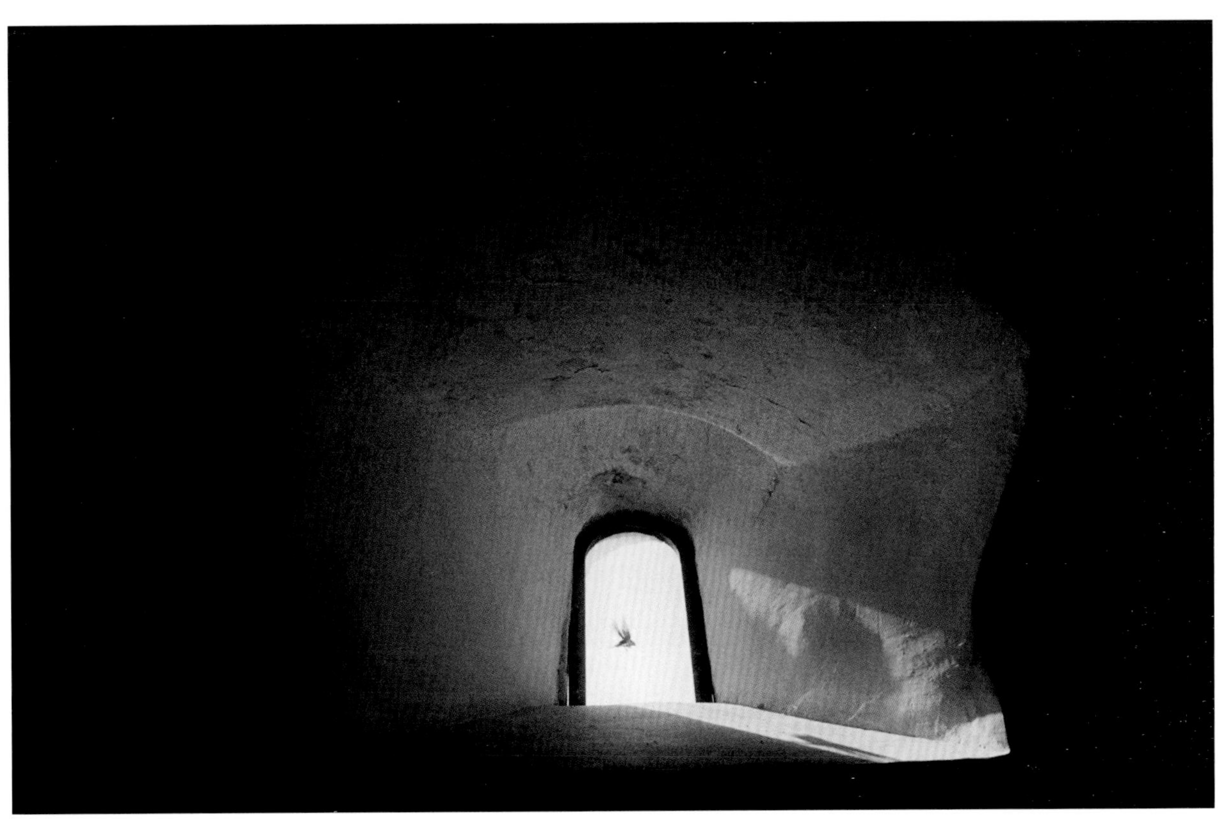

Above
Graciela Iturbide
Untitled, Actopan, Mexico, 1985

Pages 80–81
Graciela Iturbide
Pájaros en el poste (Birds on the pole),
Guanajuato, Mexico, 1990

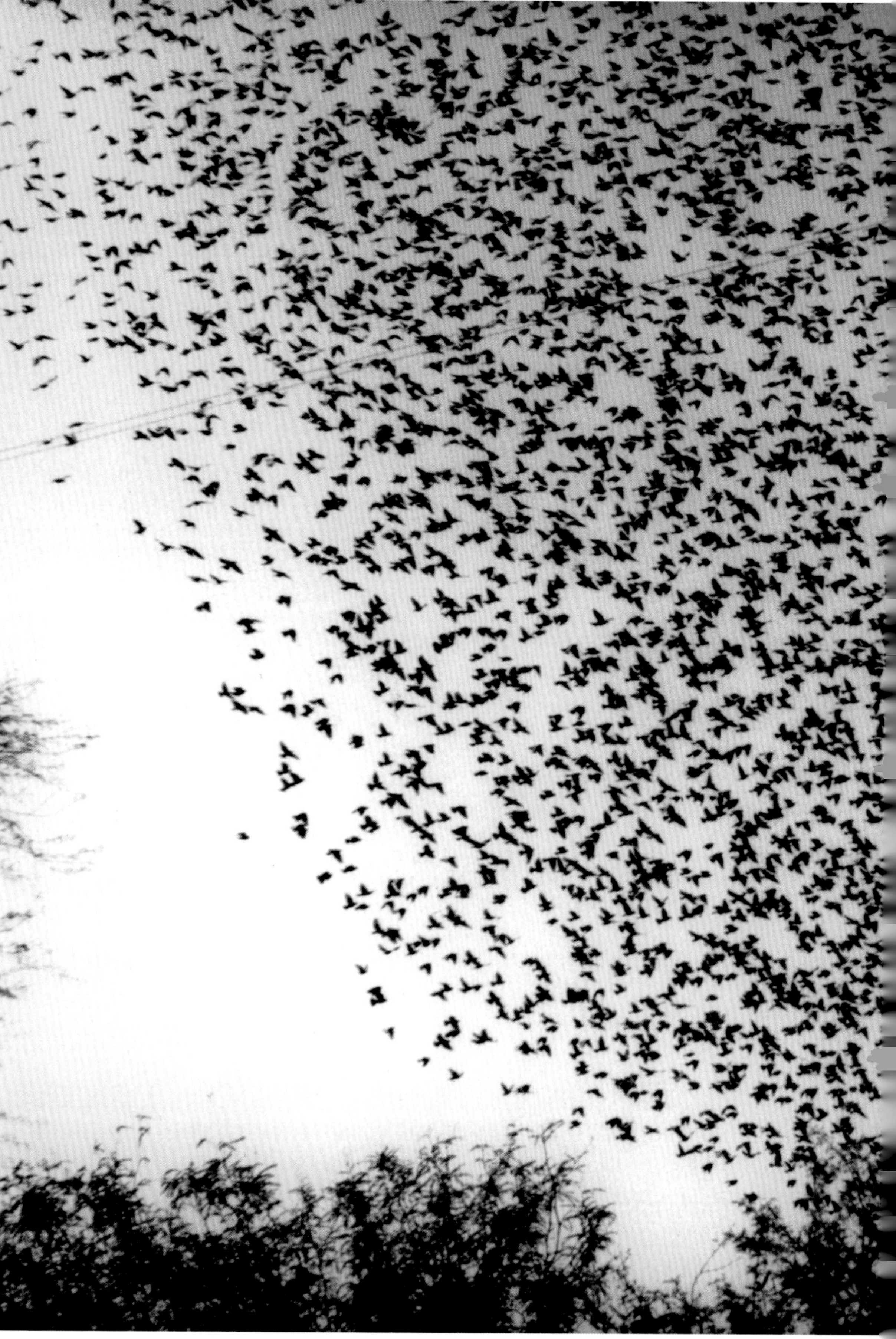

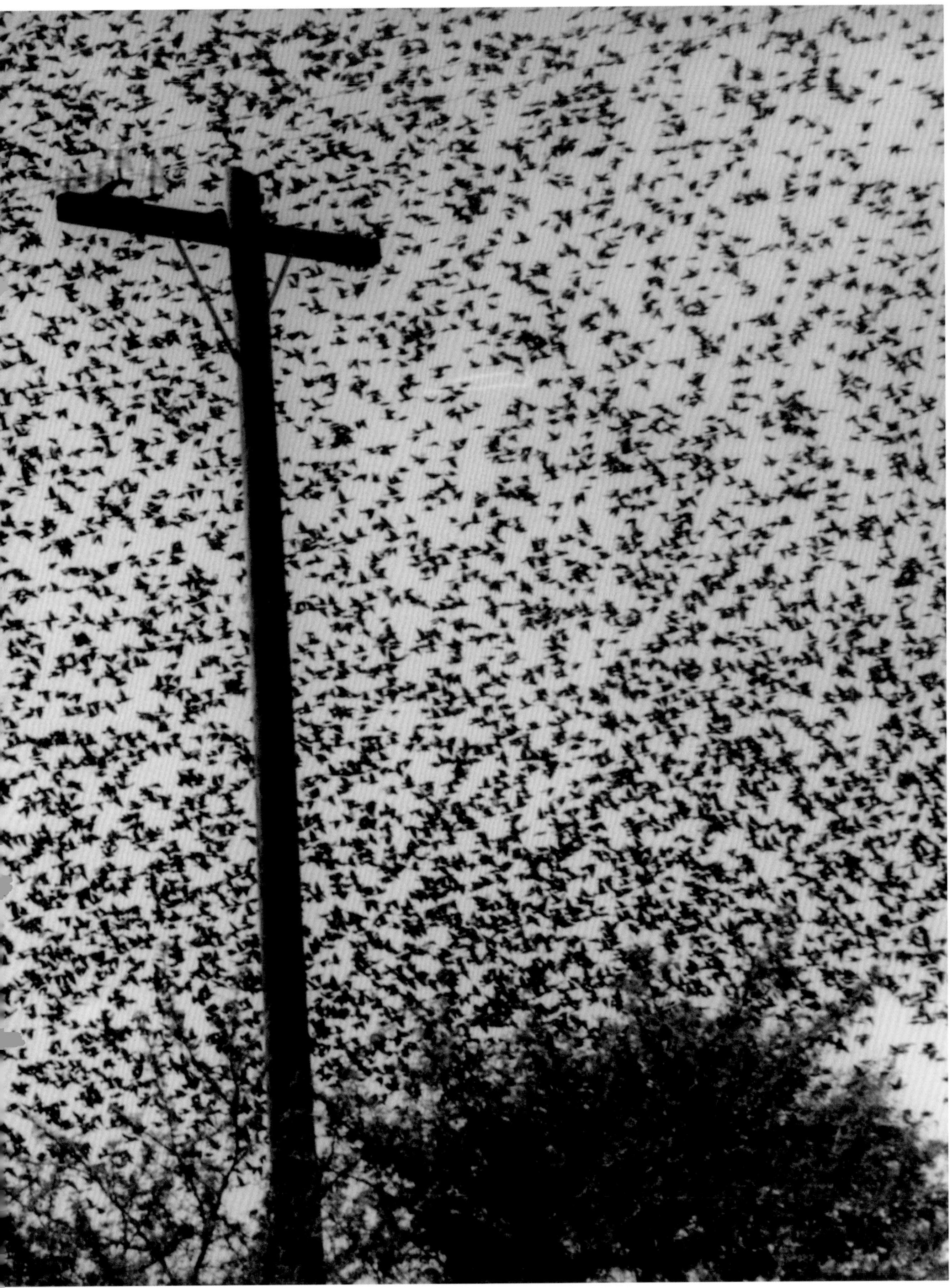

An Evanescent Witness

Self-portraiture serves as a means of questioning one's self to become more self-aware, drawing out the ideas and struggles that one carries inside. I consider it very healing. My self-portraits have always been impulsive. When something is stifling or troubling me, if an idea arises, I act on it immediately.

My first ones date back to the 1970s and were mostly my face reflected in a mirror. The self-portrait of my face decorated in the manner of the Seri people (page 9), among whom I lived in 1979, was more of a turning point as it addressed identity more directly. But it wasn't until 1989 that I began to explore the genre with more intention. I decided to use animals to infuse my self-representations with symbolic force. I have since worked with birds, snails, snakes, axolotls, and fish in order to explore my identity or express my moods.

I made the self-portrait in which I'm covering my eyes with two birds, one living and one dead, at a difficult time in my life. I had separated from my husband and moved into a little house in Coyoacán that was still in the process of being built. I had no money. I felt very fragile. I titled the photograph as a question, *Eyes to fly with?* I was wondering whether I could still continue to make photographs, whether I had the strength and enthusiasm to create new images, to fly with my eyes. The idea came to me suddenly. I took the dead bird from a drawer where I keep the strange things I find on my walks; I bought the live bird at the market. My son Mauricio helped me make the portrait. I tried variations on the theme, including ones with live birds flapping their wings.

The self-portrait in which I'm holding a fish across my mouth (page 85) was taken next to the highway on a trip from Pachuca to Mexico City. I'd bought the fish at a market. Mauricio was driving the car, night was beginning to fall. In an uninhabited area, with nothing particularly special about it, I asked him to stop. We got out, and I took the portrait. Why a fish across my mouth? I don't know. You would have to ask Freud—though the answer might be a little dangerous.

I once took a self-portrait with live snails, which are sold in the San Juan Market in Mexico City. I still get the chills remembering the trail of slime they left on my face. I don't know why I took that picture either. I don't question the impulse when it strikes.

When I was undergoing psychoanalysis, I mentioned to my analyst that I frequently imagined snakes coming out of my mouth when I was speaking. I felt the need to represent that strange sensation photographically too. I wanted to confront, through these images, manifestations of my inner world that I found unsettling.

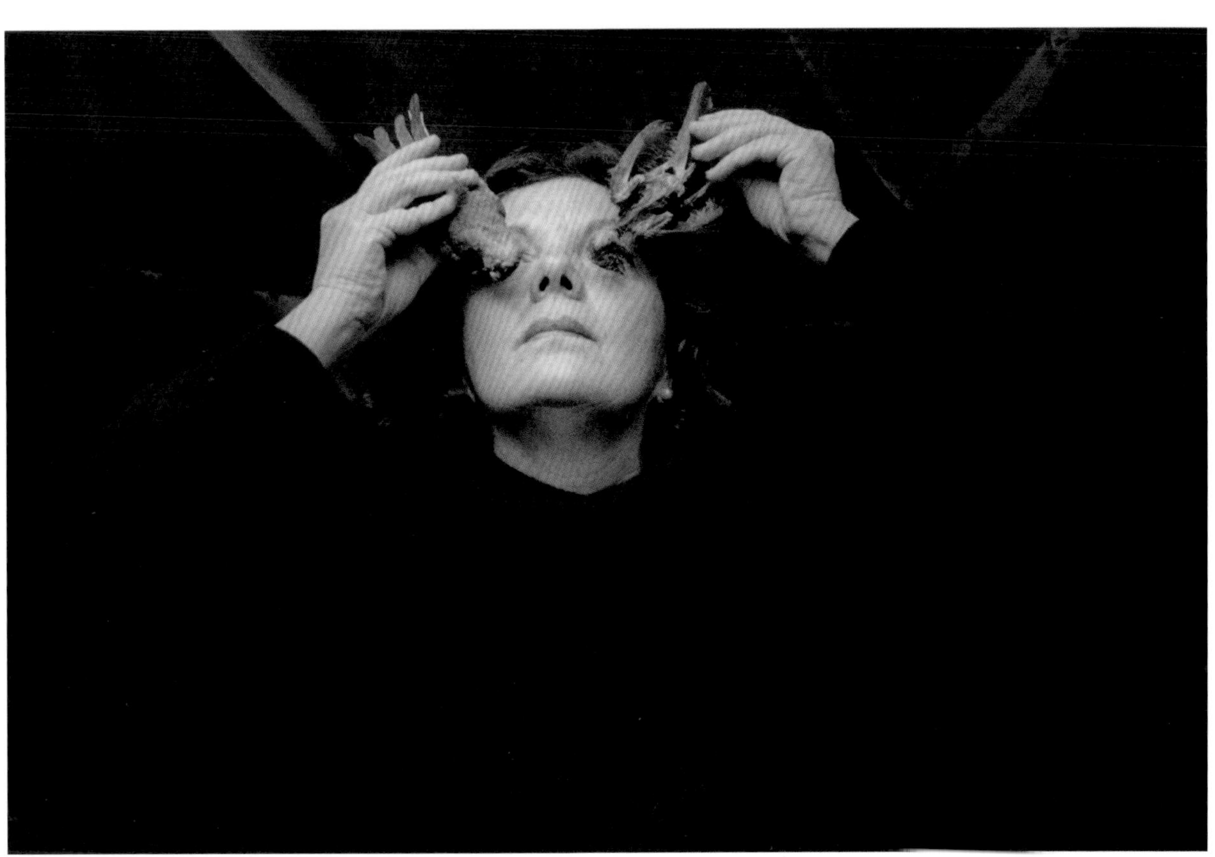

Graciela Iturbide
¿Ojos para volar? (Eyes to fly with?),
Coyoacán, Mexico City, 1991

Graciela Iturbide
Autorretrato en el campo
(Self-portrait in the countryside),
United States, 1996

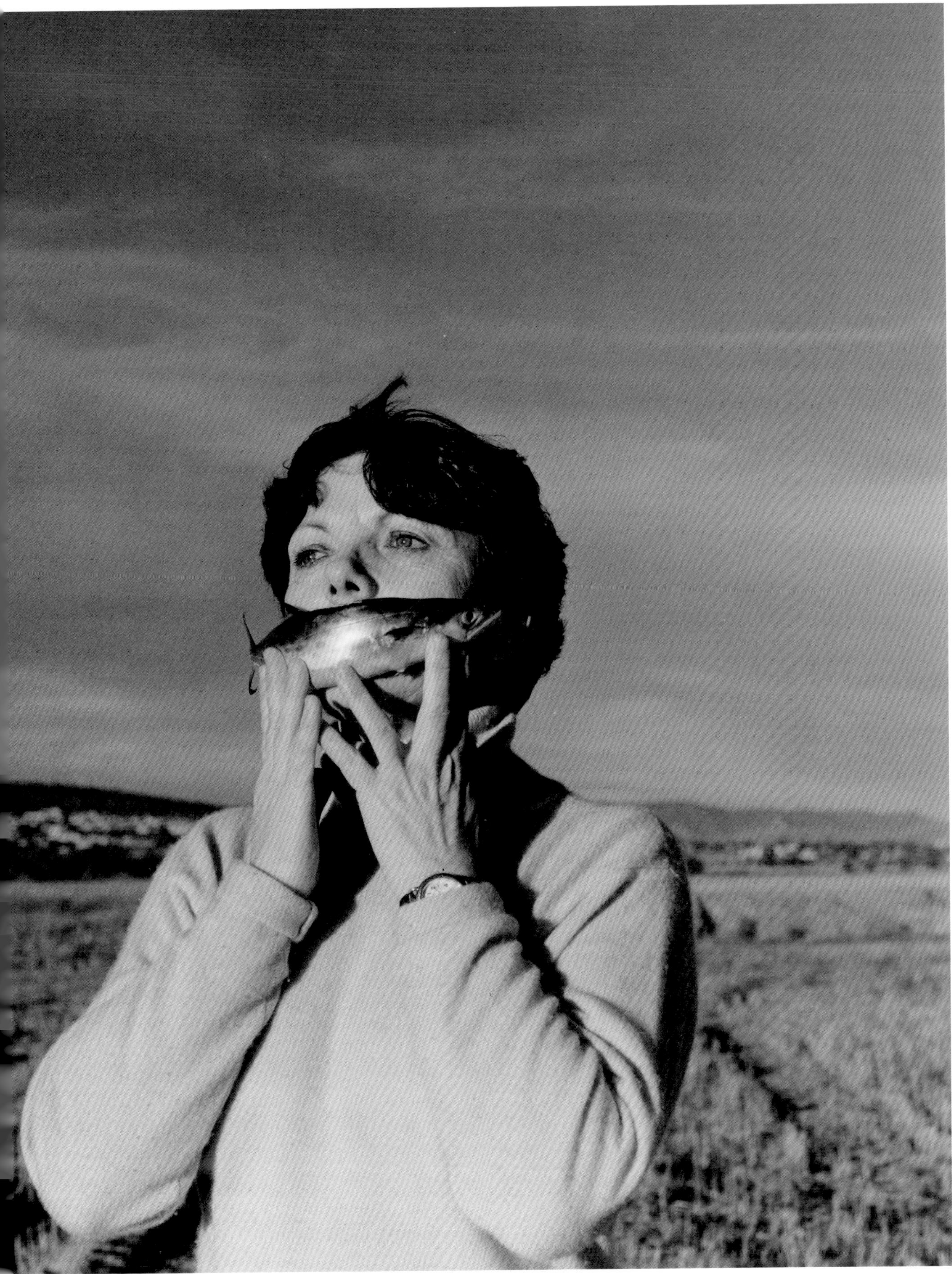

I have also made several images where I am nothing more than a shadow on a surface or landscape. The shadow as alter ego is a strategy that has been used by André Kertész and Lee Friedlander, among many other photographers whom I admire. My shadow, a blurred and evanescent witness, testifies to my passage through places that mean something to me—places penetrated with history, like the house where the revolutionary Leon Trotsky lived and died, or more personal settings like a spontaneous memorial for Francisco Toledo after his death.

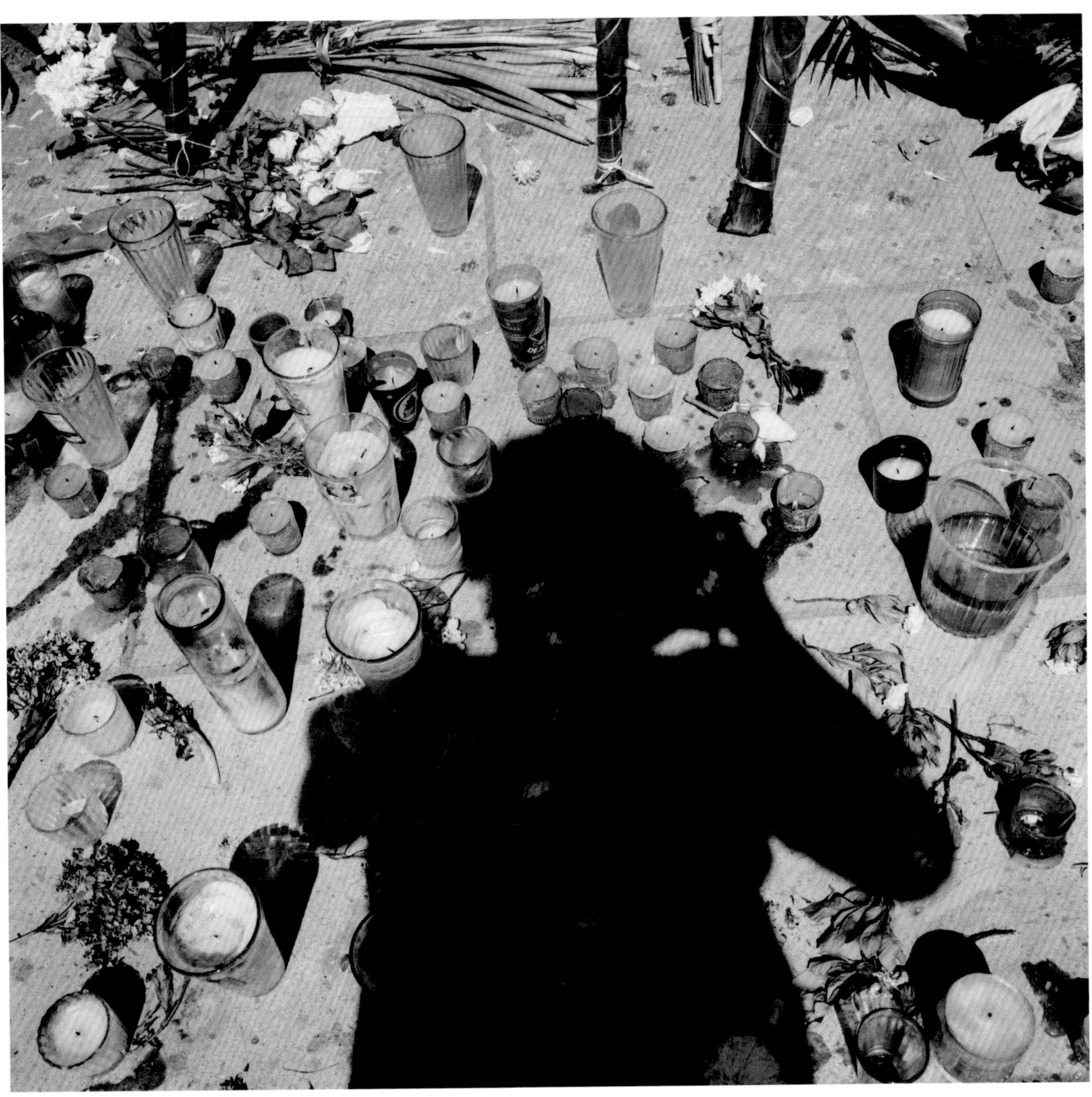

Graciela Iturbide
Autorretrato (Self-portrait),
Oaxaca, Mexico, 2019

87

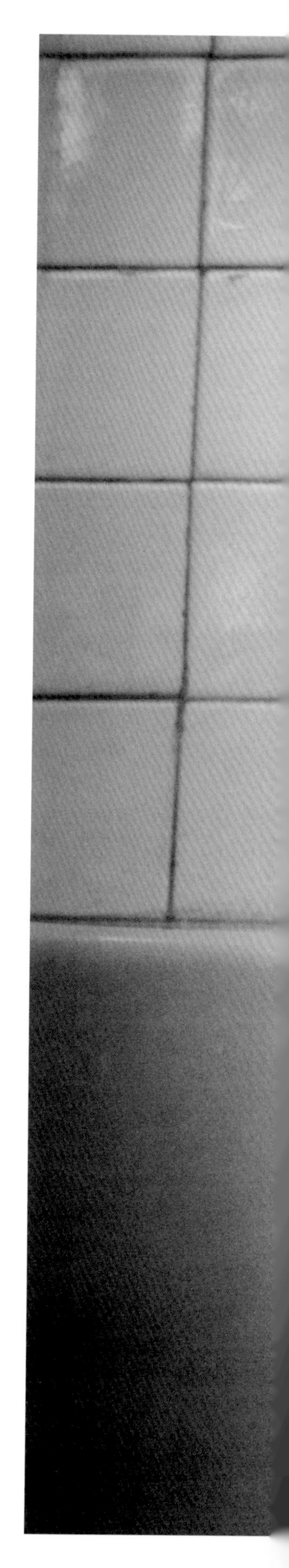

Graciela Iturbide
El baño de Frida Kahlo
(Frida Kahlo's bathroom),
Coyoacán, Mexico City, 2005

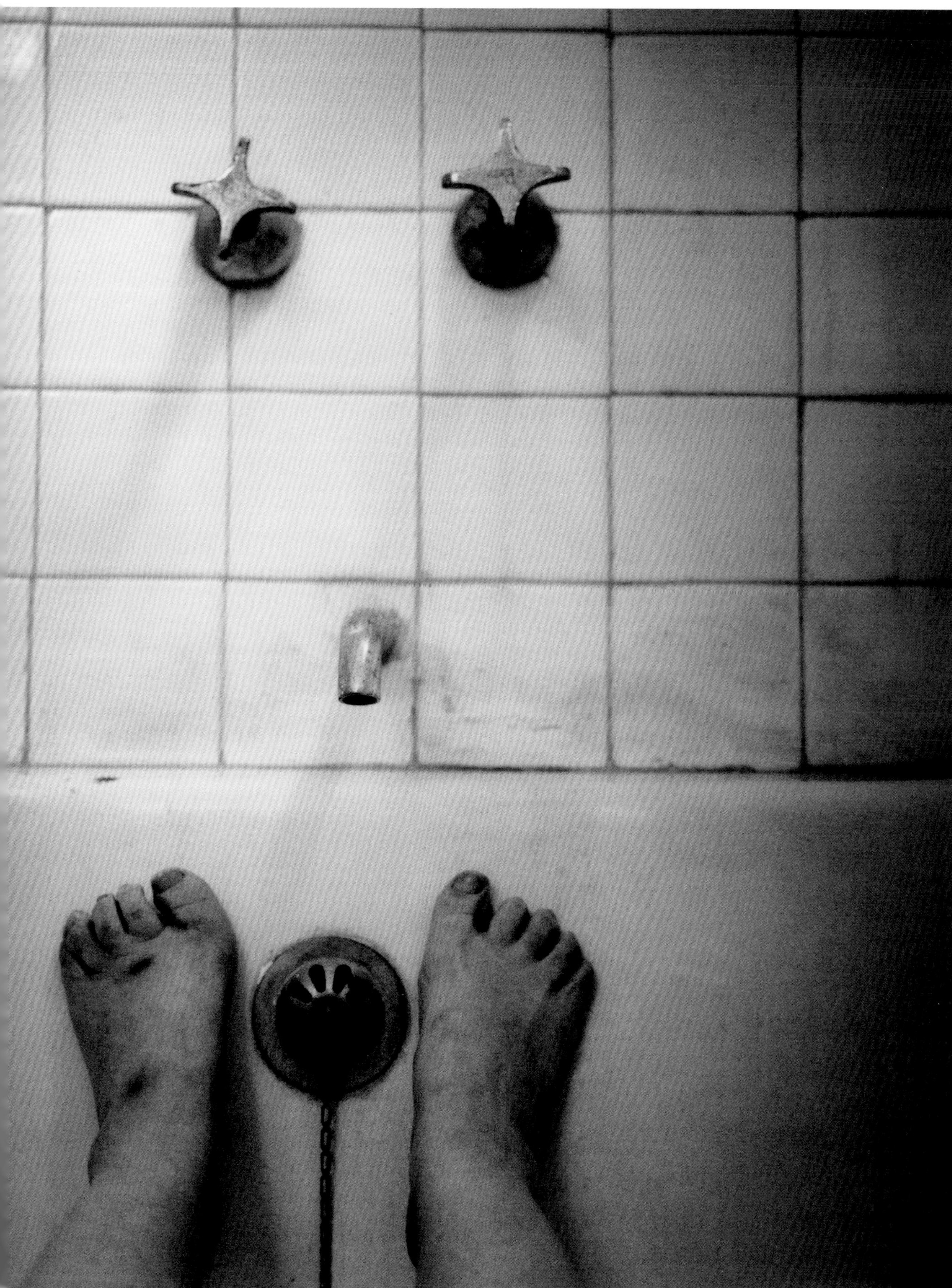

A Presence Felt

I was asked to photograph Frida Kahlo's *huipiles* (traditional tunics). They had been discovered in the private areas of Museo Frida Kahlo, also known as the Blue House. When Kahlo died in 1954, her husband, painter Diego Rivera, gave instructions that two rooms—bathrooms that had been converted into storerooms—could not be opened for fifteen years. They remained closed much longer because the head of the museum-house decided to keep them closed. It wasn't until 2002 that the objects became known: souvenirs, photographs, taxidermy, clothing, personal care and grooming products, orthopedic apparatuses connected to the physical ailments Kahlo suffered her whole life.

When I went to the Blue House to see the *huipiles*, I realized that what the museum wanted was a straightforward record of the garments. I told the director, Hilda Trujillo, that I wasn't the right photographer for the task, that I didn't take studio photos. But as I was leaving, I happened to look into one of the bathrooms and saw that a bathtub was full of miscellaneous objects, including some crutches and multiple images of Joseph Stalin. I asked permission to return and make my own work there, and Hilda agreed.

The space had a charged atmosphere, along with a strong smell and the dust of half a century. The large bottles of Demerol, the painkiller, made the biggest impression on me. Here in the bathroom was the medicine Kahlo took decades ago. I rearranged the objects in order to reinterpret the traces of her. I took photographs of enemas, Demerol, a prosthetic leg, as well as some of her corsets, which looked almost like instruments of torture. It was very moving to be in touch with her, so to speak, through photographing the objects that related to the pain she suffered. I was interested in capturing the *élan vital* of Frida Kahlo, and wanted to make a series of absent-portraits of her (recalling Manuel Álvarez Bravo's 1945 photograph where you could feel the presence of the person through only an empty gown draped across a chair). I tried to bring to life the real person rather than the celebrity.

I am not a follower of Frida's legend, not a devotee of "Fridamania"—not everything she painted appeals to me—but I acknowledge her powerful imagination and admire that her suffering did not prevent her from remaining active as an artist or a militant of leftist political causes. Her work was her therapy. I took the liberty of making a composition with my own feet in her bathtub (page 89). I later realized that this self-portrait in the tub recalled a painting of hers from 1938: *What the Water Gave Me.*

Photographs are not the only thing I have kept. Forty years ago, when I visited the house with my children (already open to the public as a museum, but not yet the place of pilgrimage it is now), I took a sprig of her sempervivum plant, which has continued to flourish today and has also produced more plants. I have thought of taking one of them back to the Blue House.

Graciela Iturbide
El baño de Frida Kahlo
(Frida Kahlo's bathroom),
Coyoacán, Mexico City, 2005

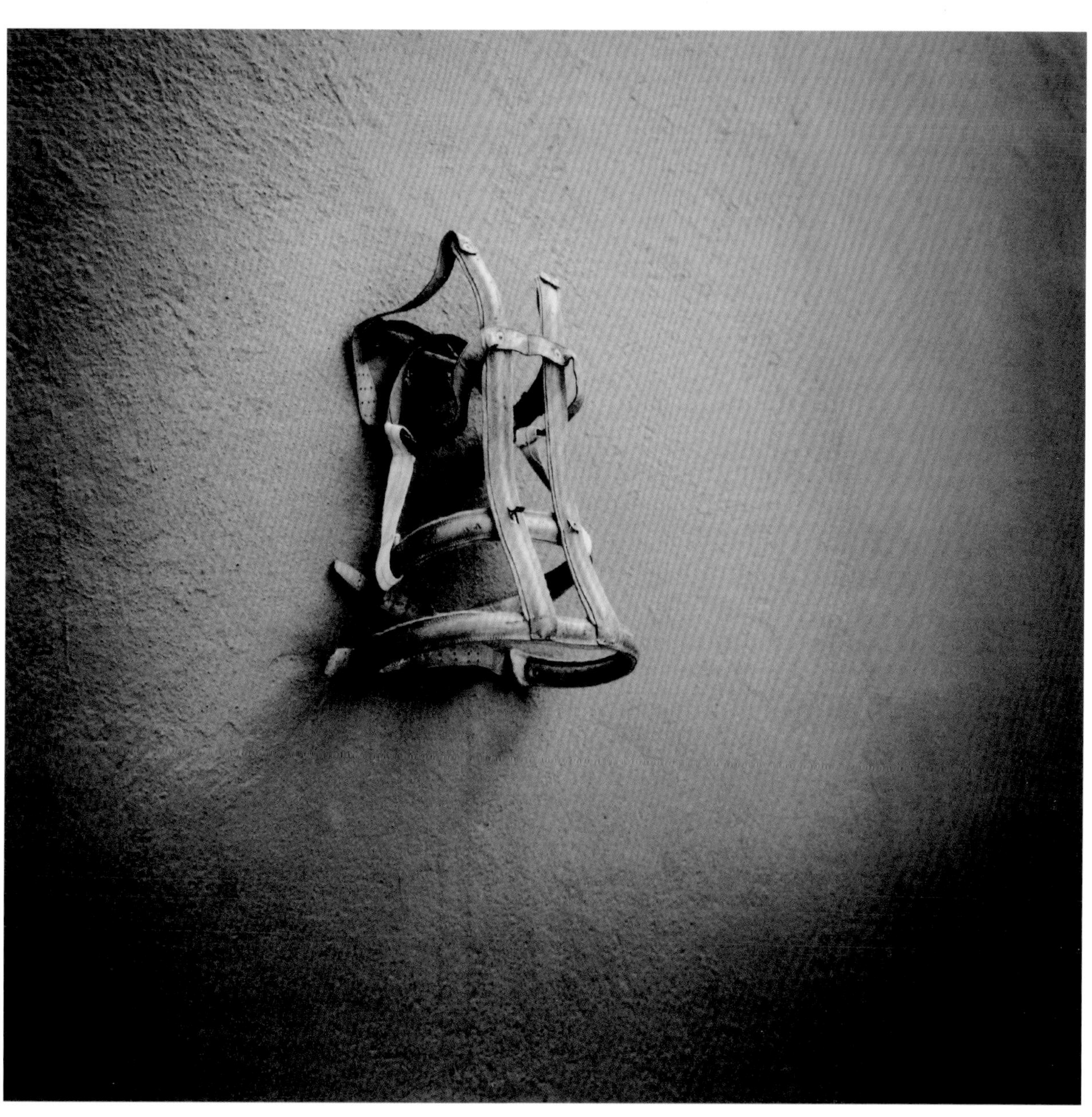

91

Other Worlds

I was changed by the knowledge that other worlds exist, both very far from and very near to my own. Through photographing, I am able to learn a little of how others see.

I have taken my camera to the different corners of our planet. Photography has given me the opportunity to get to know my own country, as well as many other places. I have made images for various reasons and purposes, some personal, some on commission for Mexican institutions such as the Instituto Nacional Indigenista or international organizations like Doctors Without Borders and the UN High Commission for Refugees. As with more personal work, the images I take during my travels express my own viewpoint, my surprise in the face of the unknown, my discovery of details that I consider significant. The images from my travels are a record from which I can reconstruct itineraries, recall the road that took me to a certain vantage point, remember the circumstances of a shot and what I felt or experienced—details not recorded photographically.

Nowadays it can feel like everything has already been photographed, that nothing escapes the fate of the tourist souvenir. It is not easy to distance oneself from preconceptions, which reinforce simplifications and stereotypes. But we must get past standardized images in order for photography (and travel) to be a way of both understanding and celebrating our differences and similarities.

It seems to me that if I embrace my authorial vision from the start, I can be honest regarding the realities of the people that I am portraying. Photography contains a regard within a regard—between the gaze of the photographer and the gaze of the subject, the image becomes a reflection of the person taking the picture. Knowing that, I try to avoid the picturesque, the exotic, or other colonial prejudices that impose the predominance of a single value system. I am interested above all in acknowledging and valuing the diversity of cultures, geographies, and contexts in which life manifests itself. I want each of my photographs to contain a little of what it means to belong to humanity.

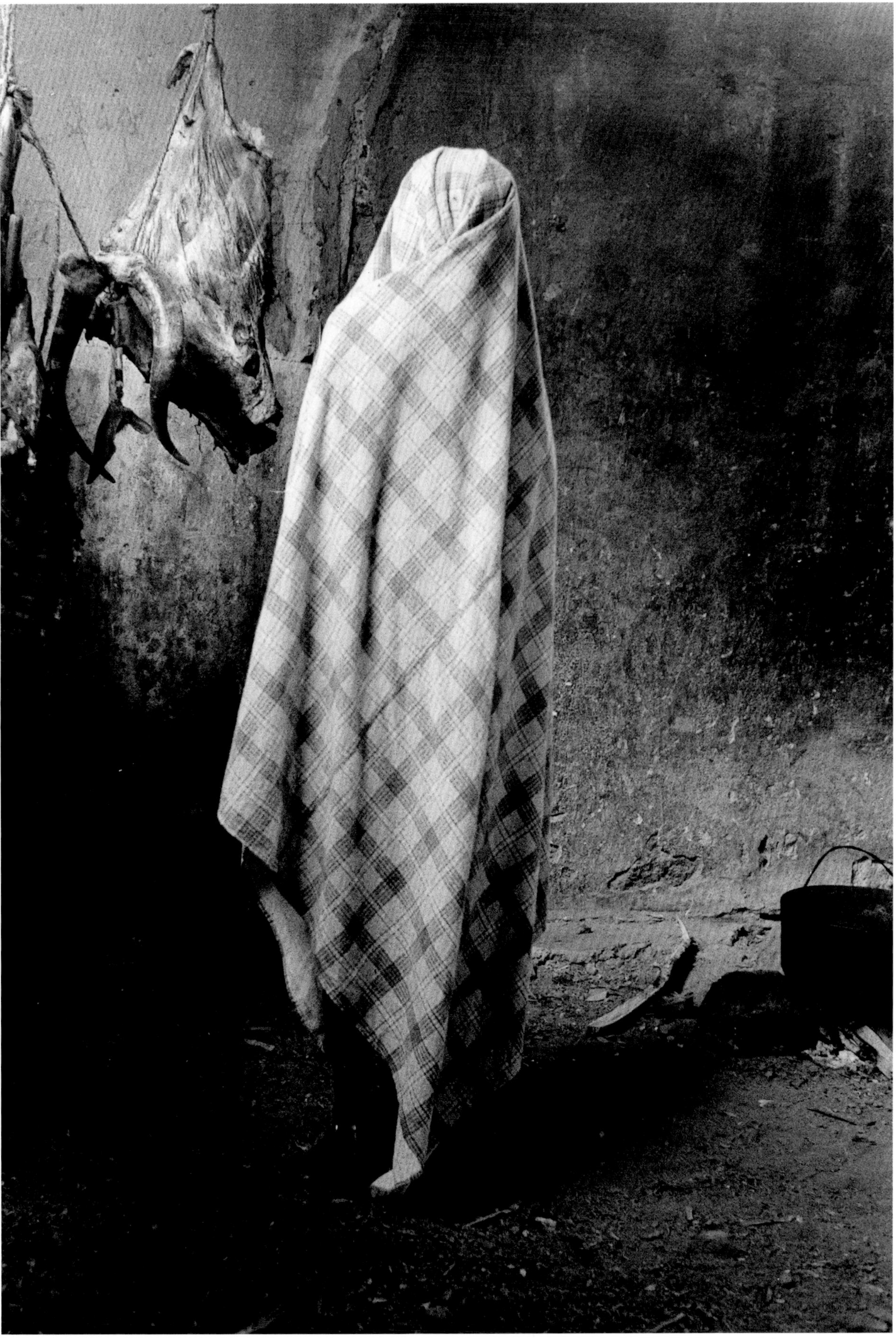

In the early 1980s, I was invited to participate in the *Day in the Life* book series, where a large group of photographers was assigned to document in a state, country, or continent, over the course of a single day. The photos were then sequenced by the hour of the day, morning to evening. I photographed for books on Ireland, the Soviet Union, Spain, the United States, and the state of California. In *A Day in the Life of America* (1986) and *A Day in the Life of California* (1988), I was more involved in choosing the subject matter. I wanted to document people of Mexican descent in California—a community of the utmost importance to the social and economic livelihood of the United States, however much this recognition is denied them.

The day chosen to take photographs for *A Day in the Life of America* was May 2, 1986. My destination was Los Angeles. Through painter Margarita García, I had arranged to photograph a group of young people known as *cholos*, which included some of her family members. Margarita took me to the house they shared in East Los Angeles. They were proud members of the White Fence Gang, which had a long history of violence in that part of California. Several of them were deaf.

For one full day and a few more hours, I lived with Lisa, Arturo, Cristina, and Rosario and her baby. I accompanied them while they met up with friends and other members of the gang, went out shopping or walked to the nearby park where drugs were sold. Their neighborhood had references to Mexican culture and identity everywhere. The women posed for me in front of a mural of three famous Mexican revolutionaries: Benito Juárez, Francisco Villa, and Emiliano Zapata. When my friend Alfredo López Austin, a great scholar of Mesoamerican civilizations, saw the image he was excited by the group's gesture to historical memory. I didn't tell him that my Angeleno friends had asked me to photograph them "by the mural of the maria-chis." Though they were mistaken about Mexican history, they still felt a profound connection to Mexico. The editors of *A Day in the Life of America* ended up choosing a portrait of several members of the group lying on a bed (pages 98–99).

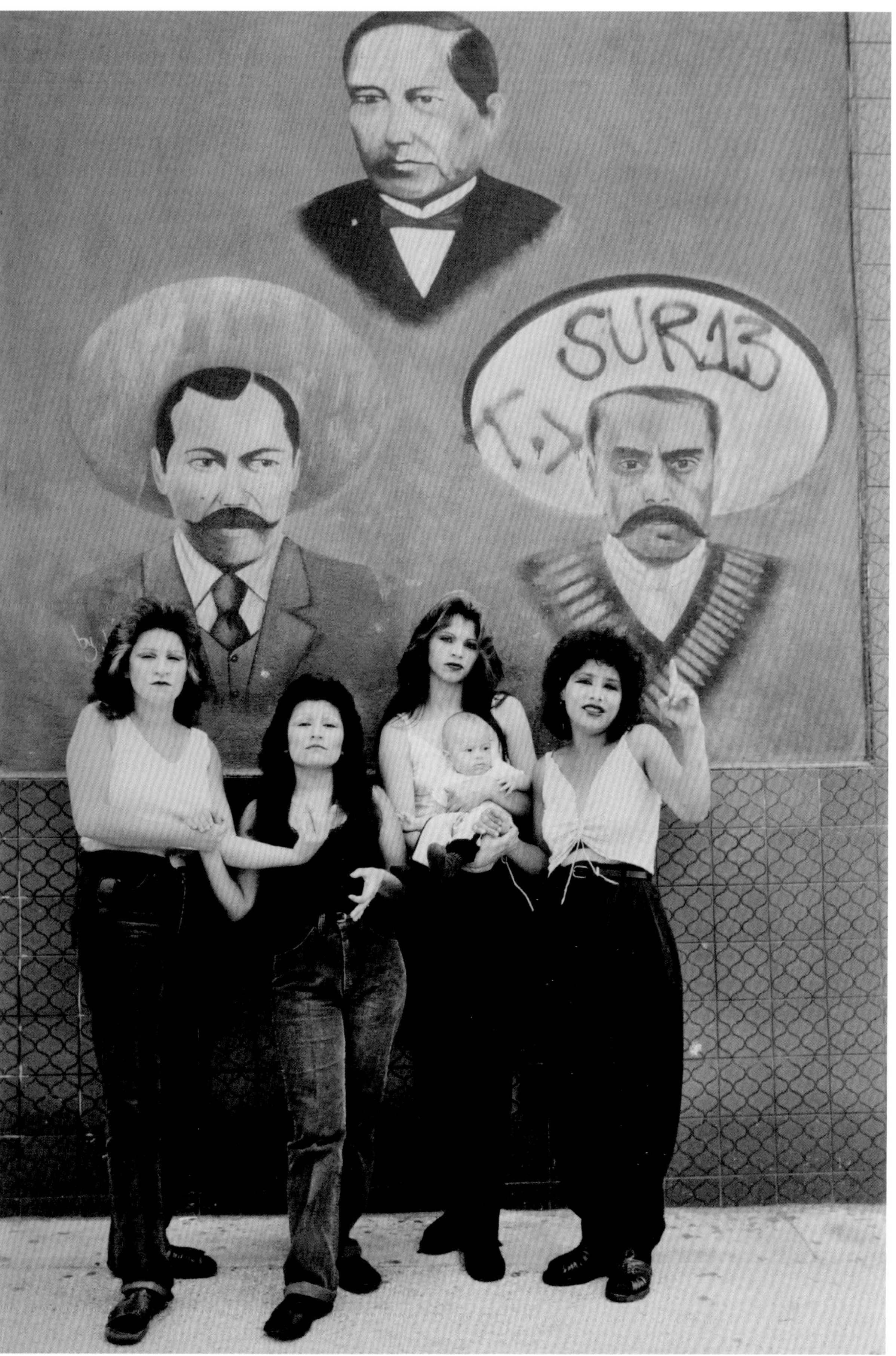

SUR 13

Although it was easy to follow a small number of people—all close friends and family—for one day, I wanted to keep photographing them, to look deeper into *cholo* culture. For this, I had to earn their trust. From the beginning, I showed them respect and made sure Lisa and her circle knew that my photographs would not show anything that went against their dignity. I avoided photographing anyone in a bad situation. Building on these relationships, I was able to continue photographing the White Fence Gang; I visited them again in 1989 and made portraits of the original subjects, as well as of other friends and family members.

I had no contact with the group again until 2007, when some of them came to the opening of an exhibition of mine, *The Goat's Dance*, at the J. Paul Getty Museum. After seeing their younger selves, they invited me to come back to make more pictures. With the help of Margarita García, I was able to locate many of the people I had photographed in the 1980s. I made several trips to extend the series to show where their lives had taken them and include their widening familes with many children and grandchildren. On my last visits in 2018 and 2019, I saw Lisa at a Dodgers party with family and friends, and later in a hospital bed, and then finally in portraits displayed at her graveside on the one year anniversary of her death. I was only able to photograph Rosario on the screen of a smartphone, like an apparition. This marked the end of the project. I was pleased to have been part of their lives and to know that the portraits I took of Lisa and Rosario had become a part of their children and grandchildren's memories.

There is a Jean Cocteau quote about cinema, but I like it for photography. "The only way to kill death is photography." An image remains with family, in memory, in an exhibition or a book—in history.

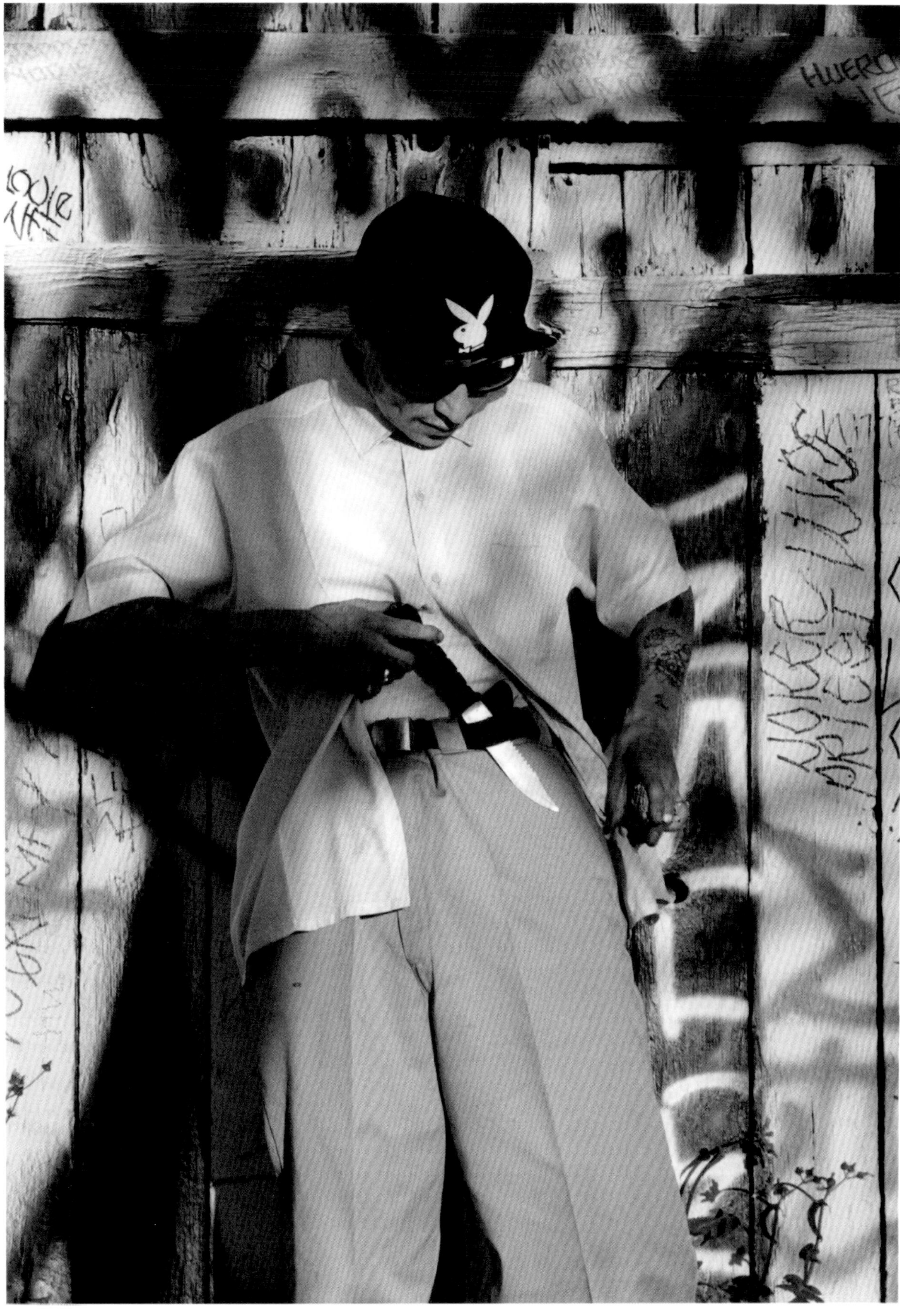

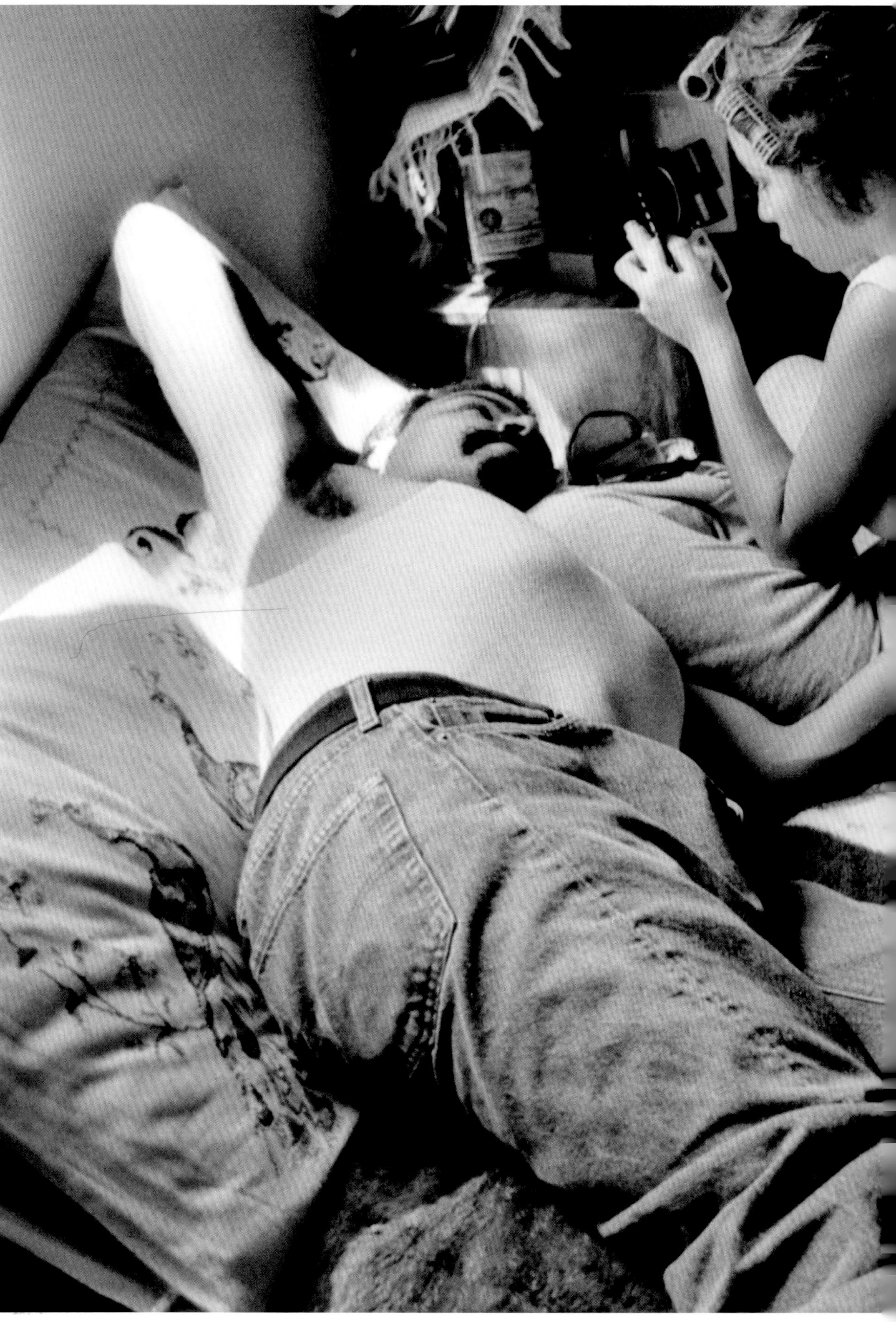

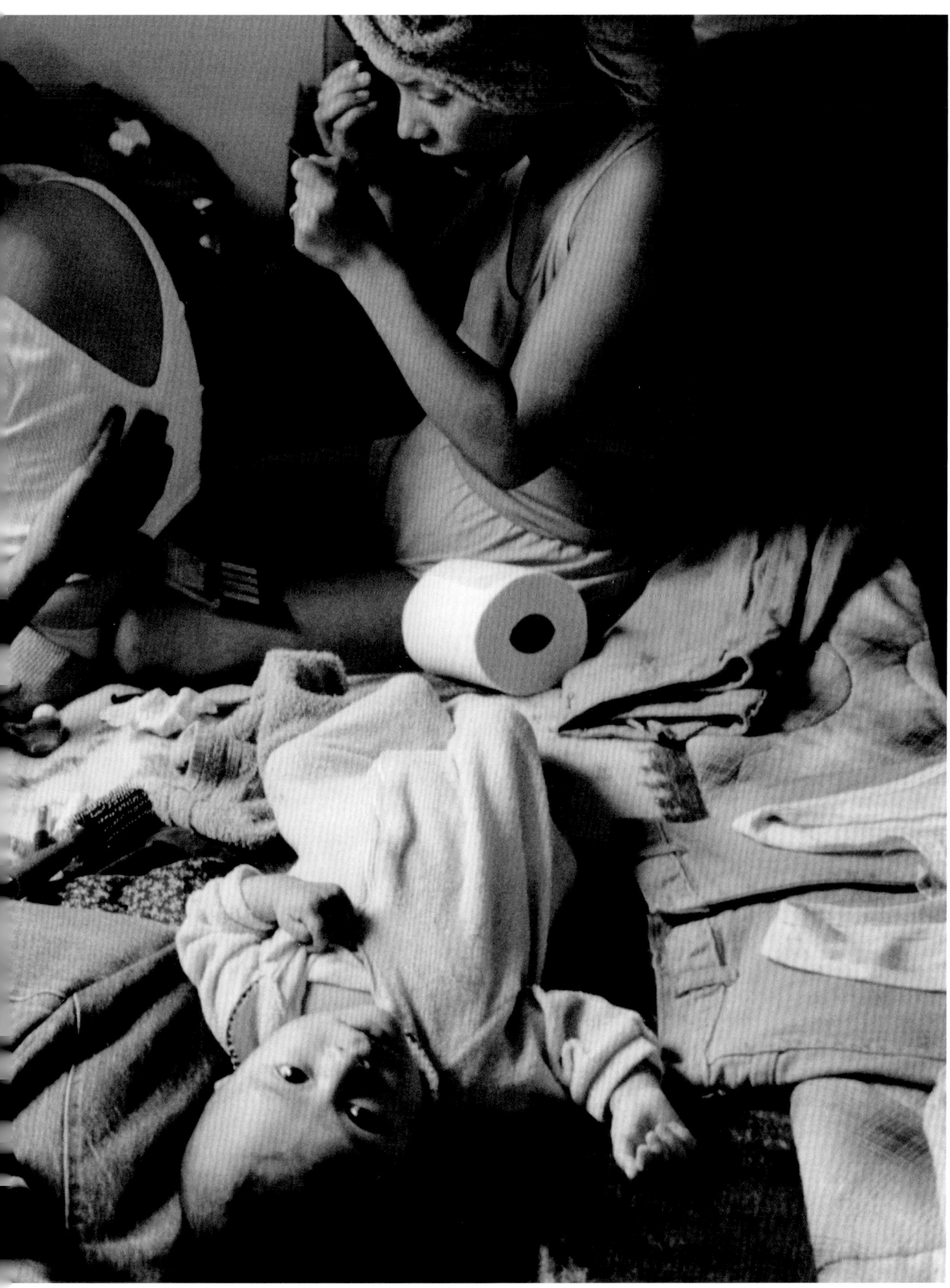

I first became interested in landscape as a genre during a road trip in the United States. The trip came about because a collector wanted to purchase photographs, but wanted them to be of the United States. Through Rose Gallery, he commissioned me with poet and friend Roberto Tejada to make the trip; I would take the pictures, and Roberto would write the poems. Roberto and I left Mexico together, heading for New Orleans. For three weeks we visited places in the Deep South, driving along the Mississippi River. We traveled on country roads, off the main highways. Whenever I saw something that interested me, I would say, "Roberto, stop, stop," because he did all the driving. We stayed in hotels we came across along the way and ate very well using a Creole restaurant guide. We went to visit photographer William Eggleston and to Elvis Presley's house, Graceland, in Memphis. We even met up with a tornado.

I was captivated by the solitude of the United States from the road and invigorated by photographing the landscape, which was so contrary to the way I had worked before, immersed as I usually am in people and how they live. I was on a new quest and began to see things I had never taken the time to pay attention to before.

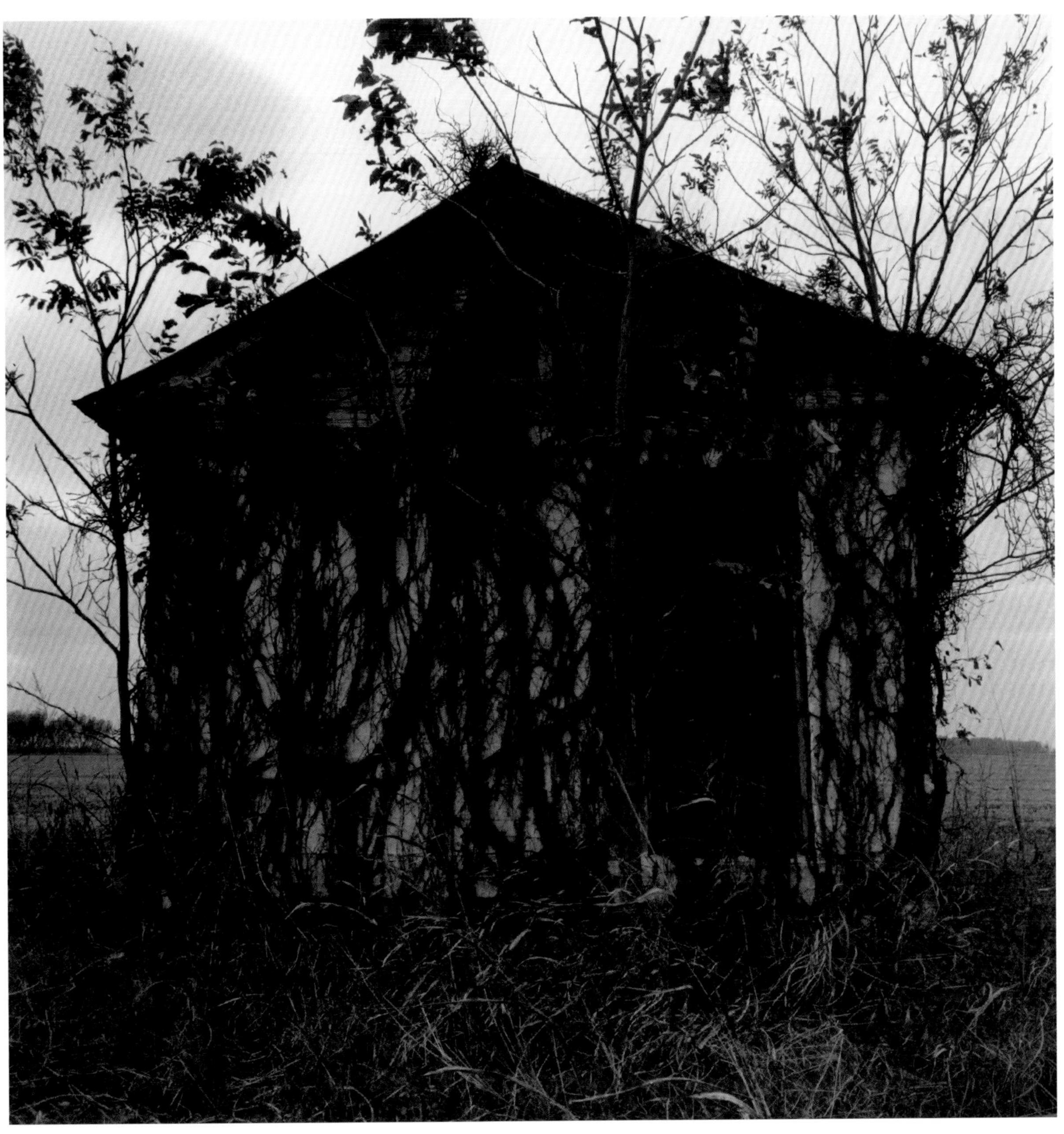

Graciela Iturbide
Carretera 61: De Memphis,
Tennessee a Clarksdale, Mississippi
(Highway 61: From Memphis,
Tennessee to Clarksdale,
Mississippi), 1997

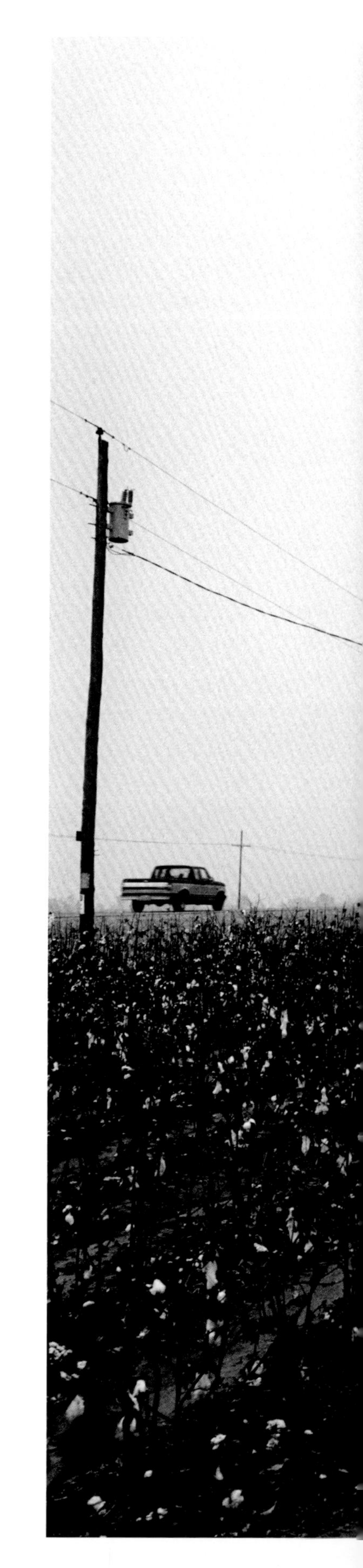

Graciela Iturbide
Carretera 61: De Clarksdale,
Mississippi a Memphis, Tennessee
(Highway 61: From Clarksdale,
Mississippi to Memphis,
Tennessee), 1997

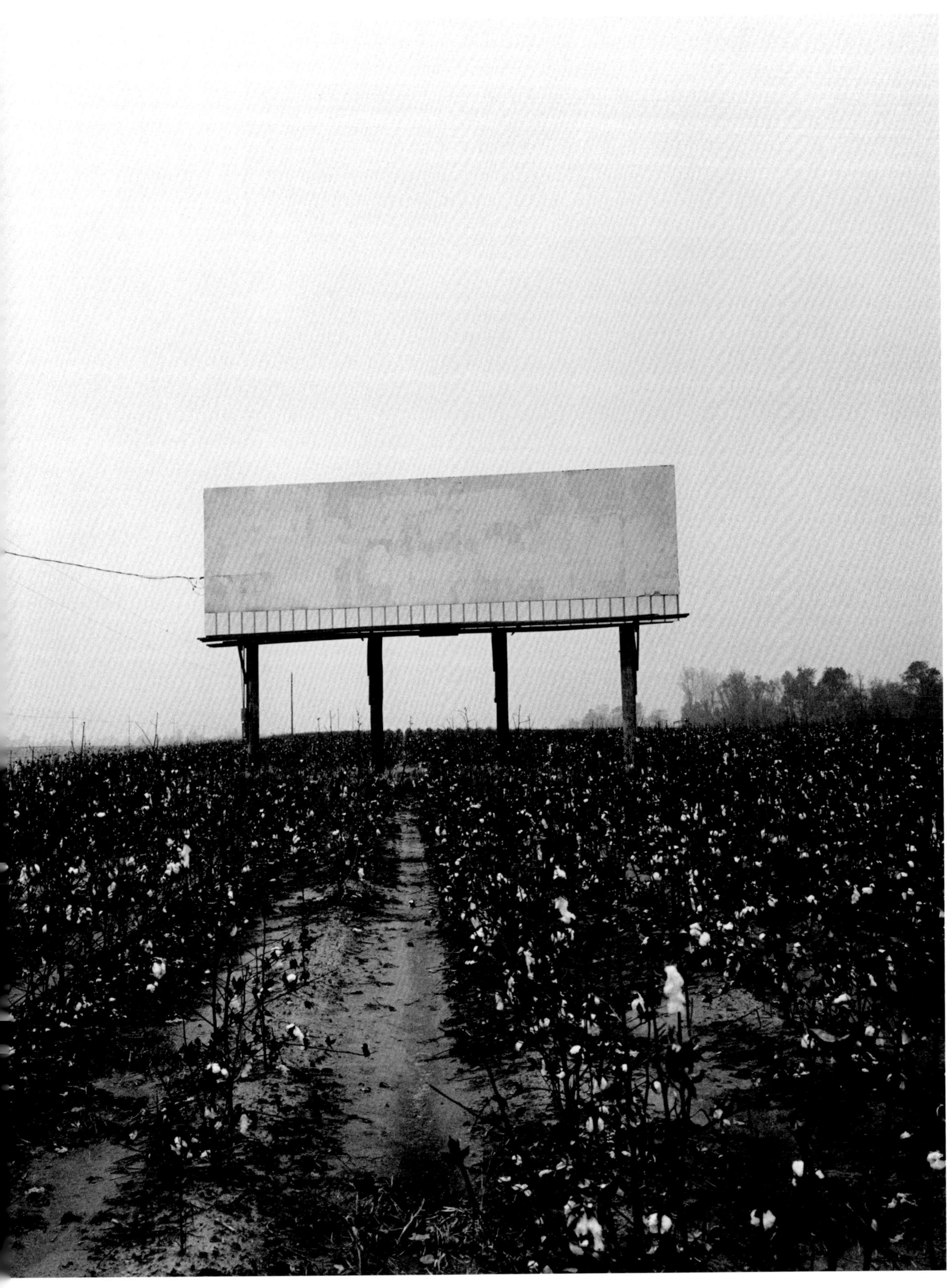

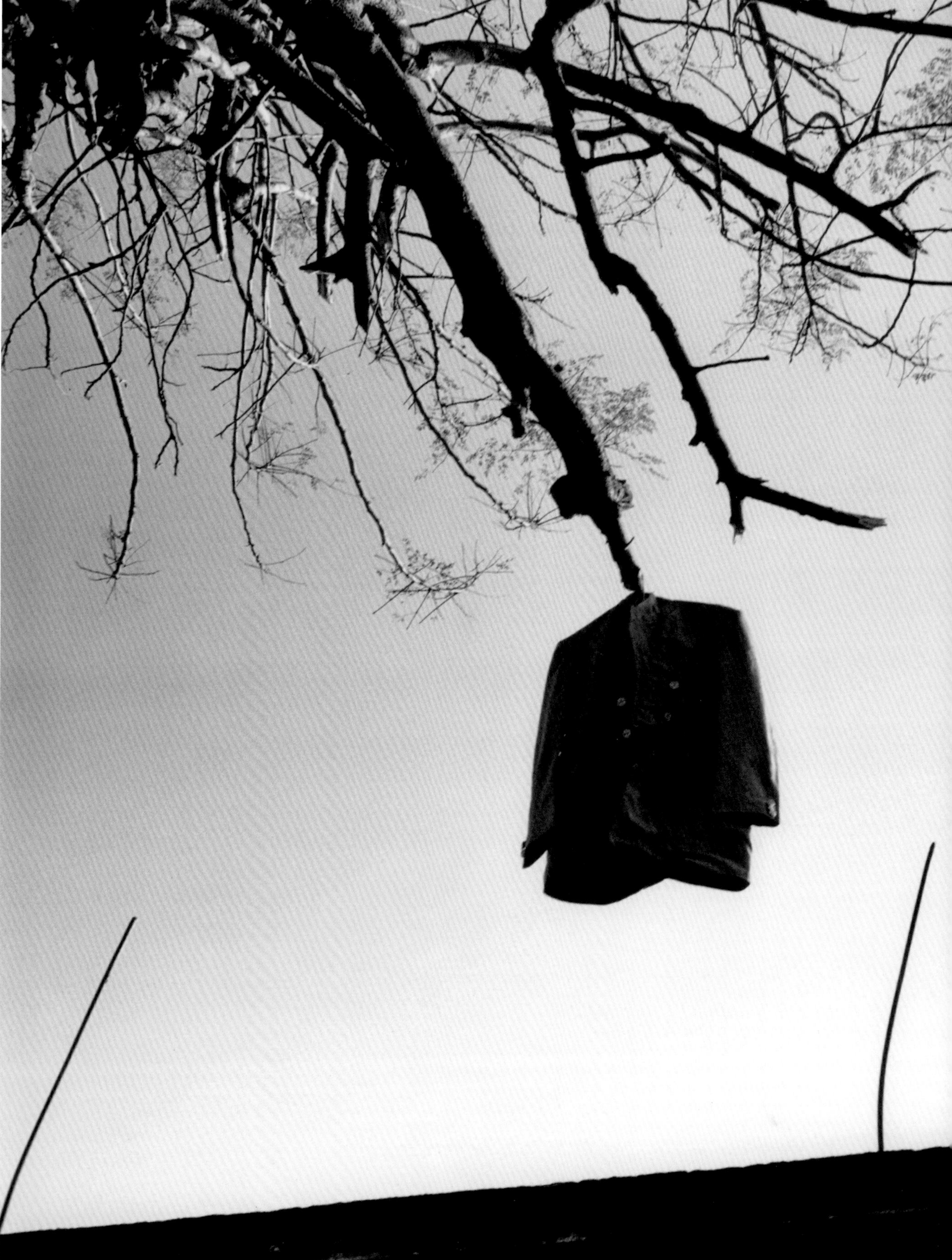

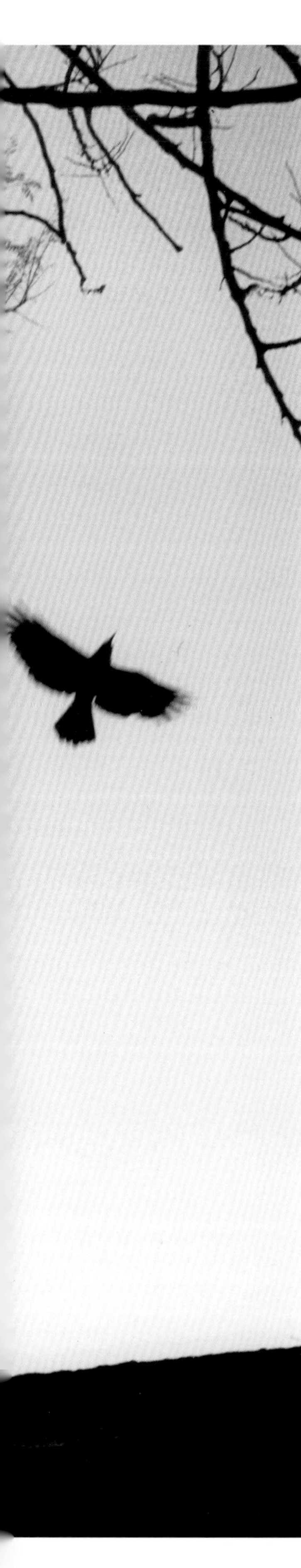

Graciela Iturbide
Untitled, Khajuraho, India, 1998

As it happened, I left for India shortly after being in the United States. If I had
gone to India ten years earlier, I may have been indifferent to the landscape, but
my American road trip had so influenced my eye, that when I arrived in India I was
drawn to the jacket hanging from a tree (page 104).

I have since been to India five times—I see certain echoes of Mexico there,
and that filters my experience too. When I arrived in Rishikesh, it reminded me
of the little village of Chalma in Mexico. I saw the same kitsch Christ figures, but they
had the features of Shiva. I never want to fall into the clichés of what has already
been photographed, including in India. I look for other things that haven't
appeared in books or the media. For instance, I photographed the *Times of India*
spread out on the ground under bowls for collecting alms rather than the beggar
(page 108). And I look for things that have symbolic meaning for me: I saw the
hand of Fatima, the symbol of the Communist Party, everywhere in Kolkata.

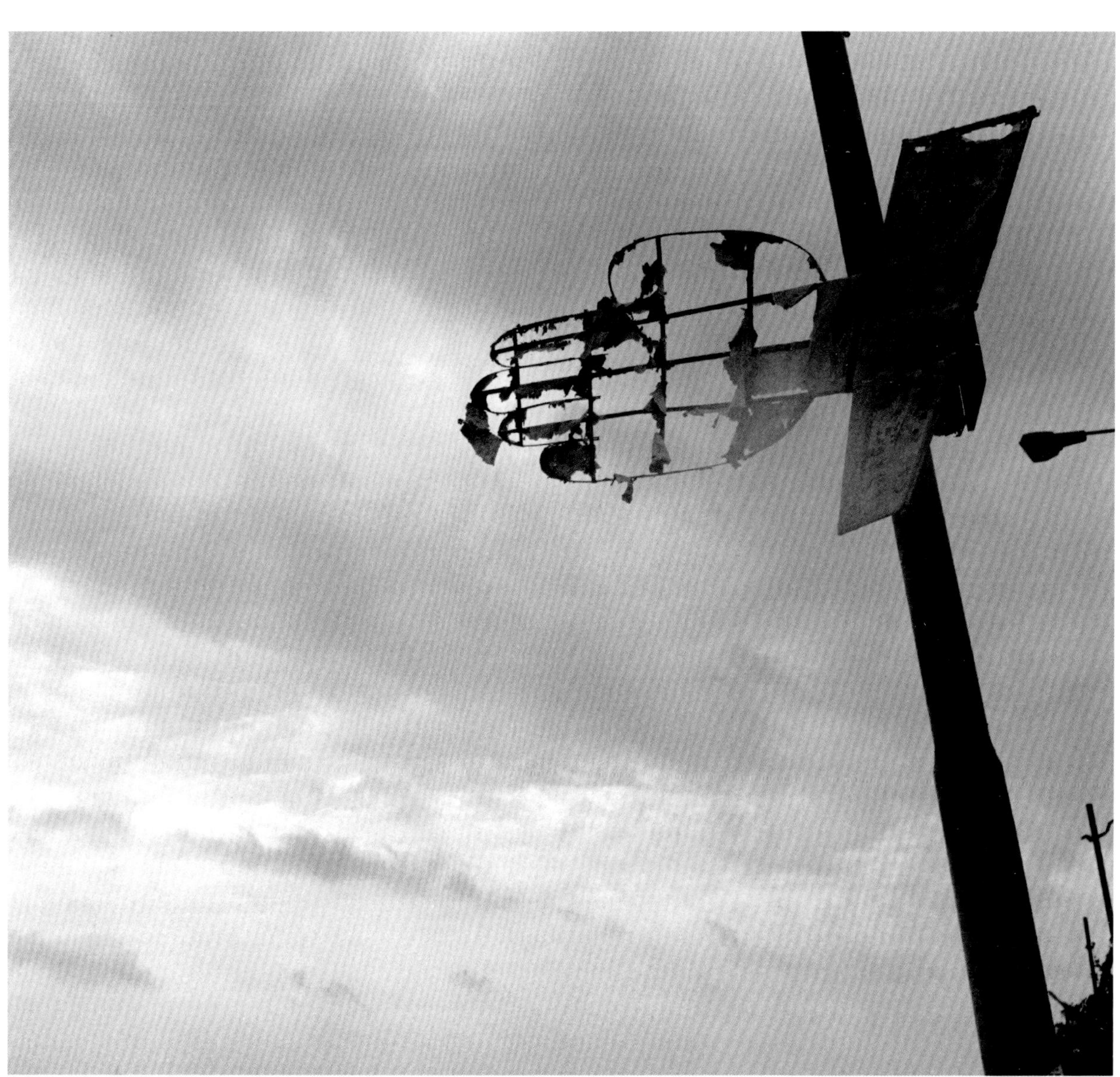

Graciela Iturbide
Untitled, Kolkata, India, 1999

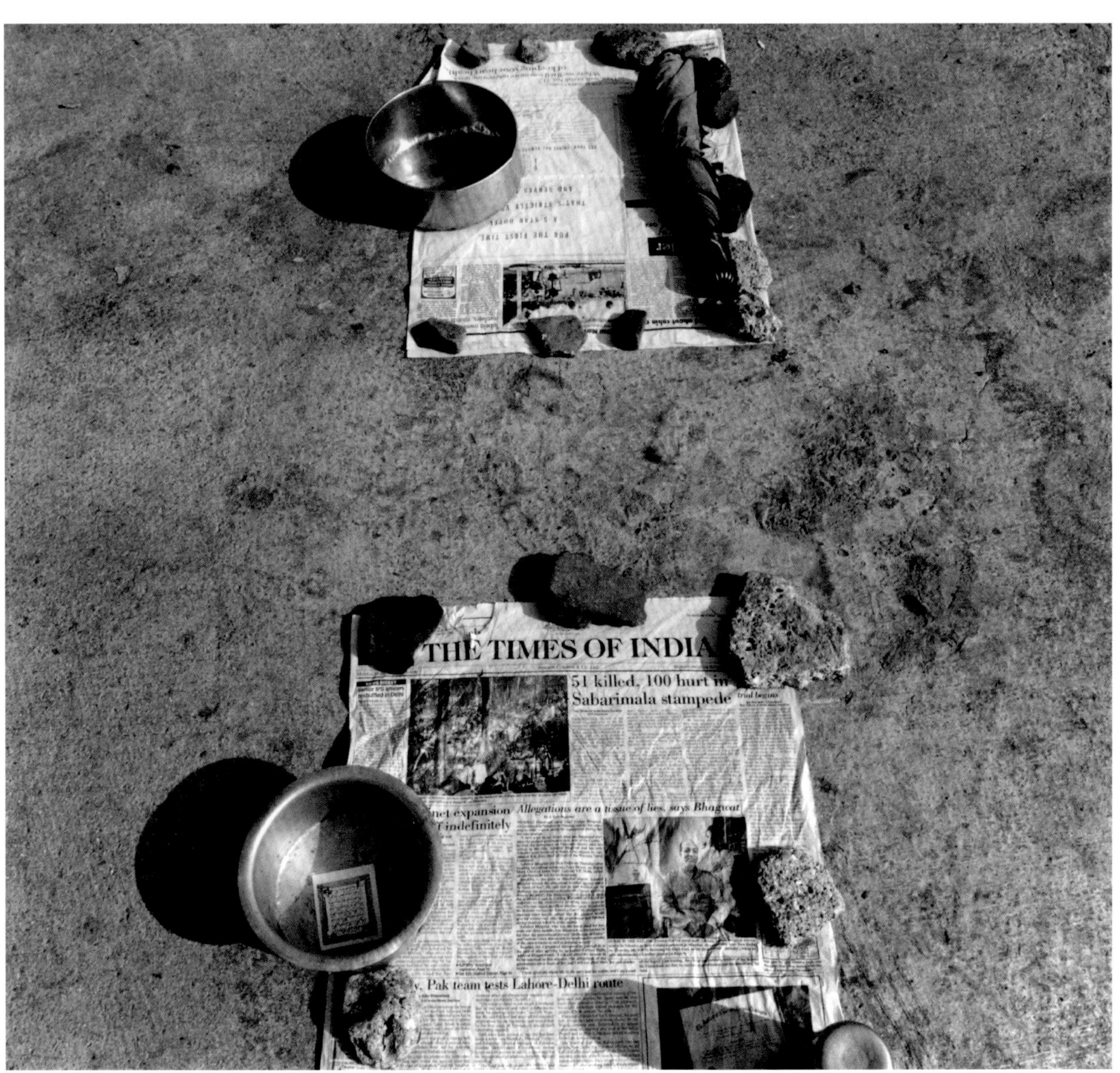

Graciela Iturbide
The Times of India,
Mumbai, India, 1999

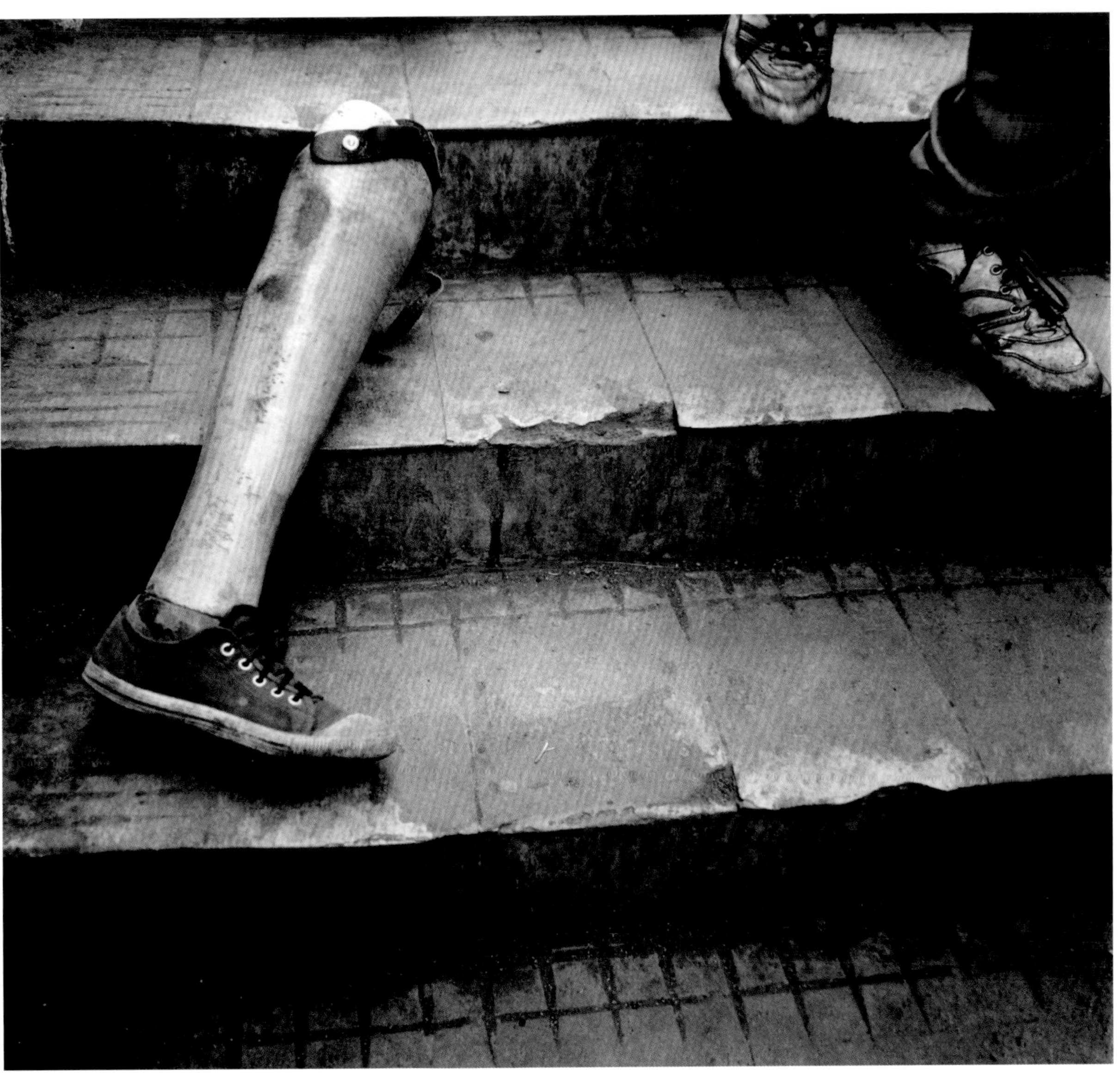

109

The Gardener

For me, the natural world is a source of both beauty and knowledge. Even the tiniest garden is a living encyclopedia that informs all the senses. There is an order and harmony in the forms and textures of plant life that photography can help us decipher.

When Francisco Toledo invited me to take photographs in the botanical gardens of Oaxaca, I said, "What's left to do with plants? Karl Blossfeldt has done it all already." "Just come, Graciela, just come," Francisco said. The place made me crazy with delight. I was fortunate enough to photograph the garden while it was still under construction and not open to the public. I captured the plants, many relocated from around the region, while they were in therapy, so to speak. They were held up by strings, stakes, and structures—the gardener's caretaking is visible, though the gardener is never seen. I had access to the grounds at any hour and photographed the plants for several months.

Though gardens and landscapes remain in one place, they are never the same. They change with the seasons, the time of day, the light that illuminates them, the vantage point from which we observe them. Gardens have made me sensitive to nature's cyclical transformations, small and large. Observing and contemplating the life of a garden can help us understand that we occupy a modest place within the vastness of nature.

I have had the opportunity to photograph botanical gardens in other parts of the world since then, in India, the United States, Brazil, and Italy. Gardens are always the product of both nature and culture. They can also be spaces of fantasy and dreams, like the Gardens of Bomarzo in Italy built in the sixteenth century by Pier Francesco Orsini. Orsini intended the gardens as an homage to his late wife— his guide was the *Hypnerotomachia Poliphili*, an allegorical work with woodcuts that narrates the dream of Poliphilus, who is searching for his beloved. I photographed the fantastical constructions and mythological figures that populate the garden, all of which emerged from that dream world: sphinxes, nymphs, furies, a dragon, pegasus, and a leaning house, among others. It is not only plants that take root in the fertile soil of gardens, but also allegories, metaphors, and imagination.

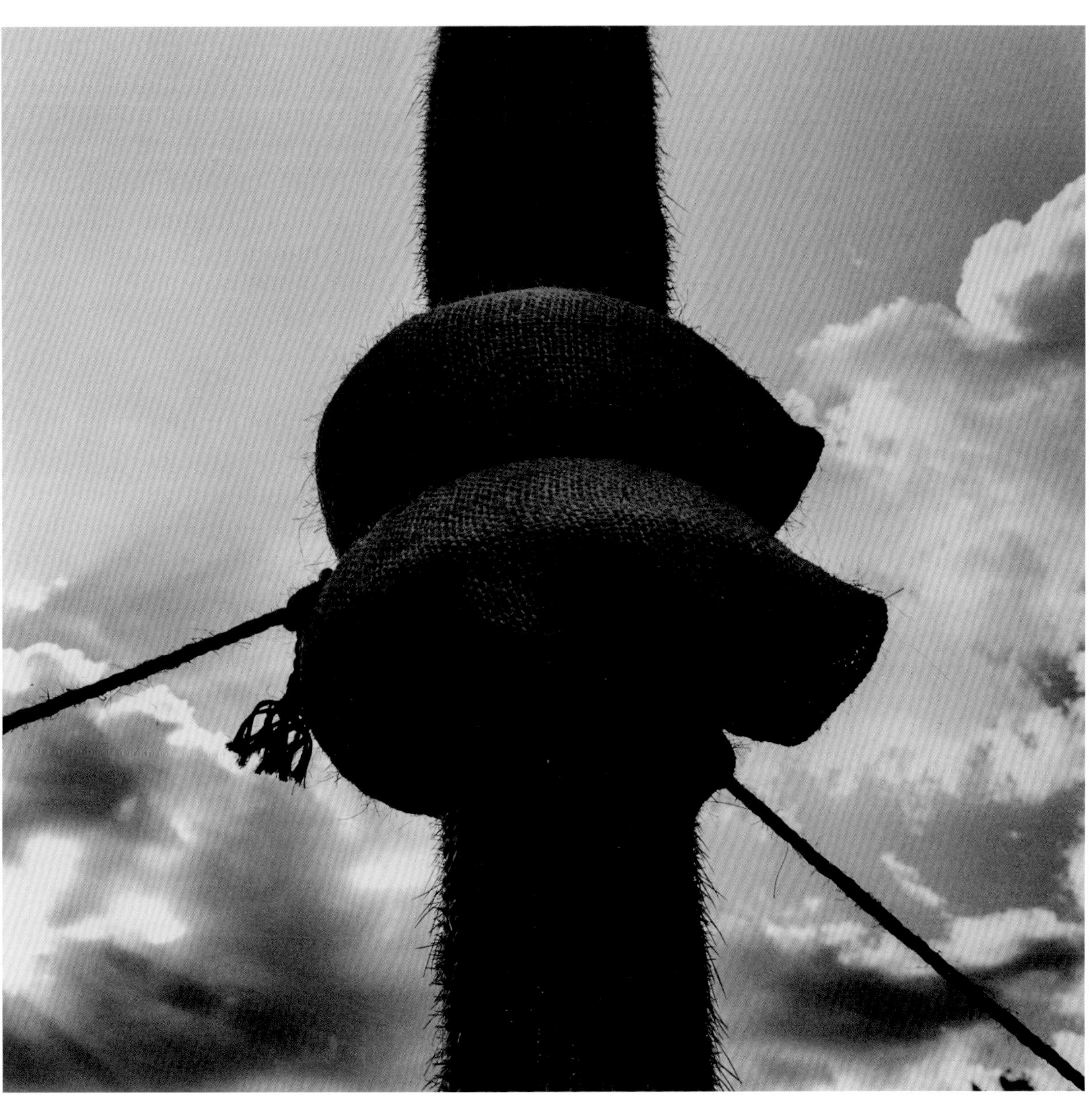

Graciela Iturbide
Jardín Botánico (Botanical Garden),
Oaxaca, Mexico, 1998–99

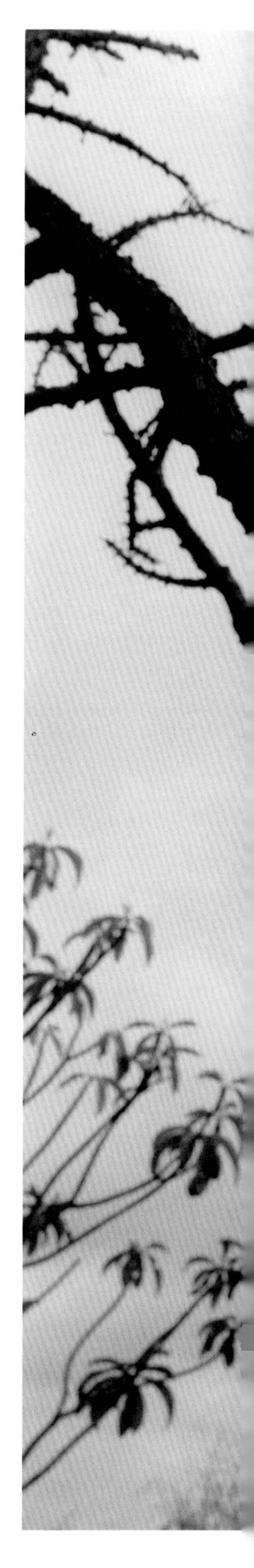

Graciela Iturbide
Jardín Botánico (Botanical Garden),
Oaxaca, Mexico, 2000

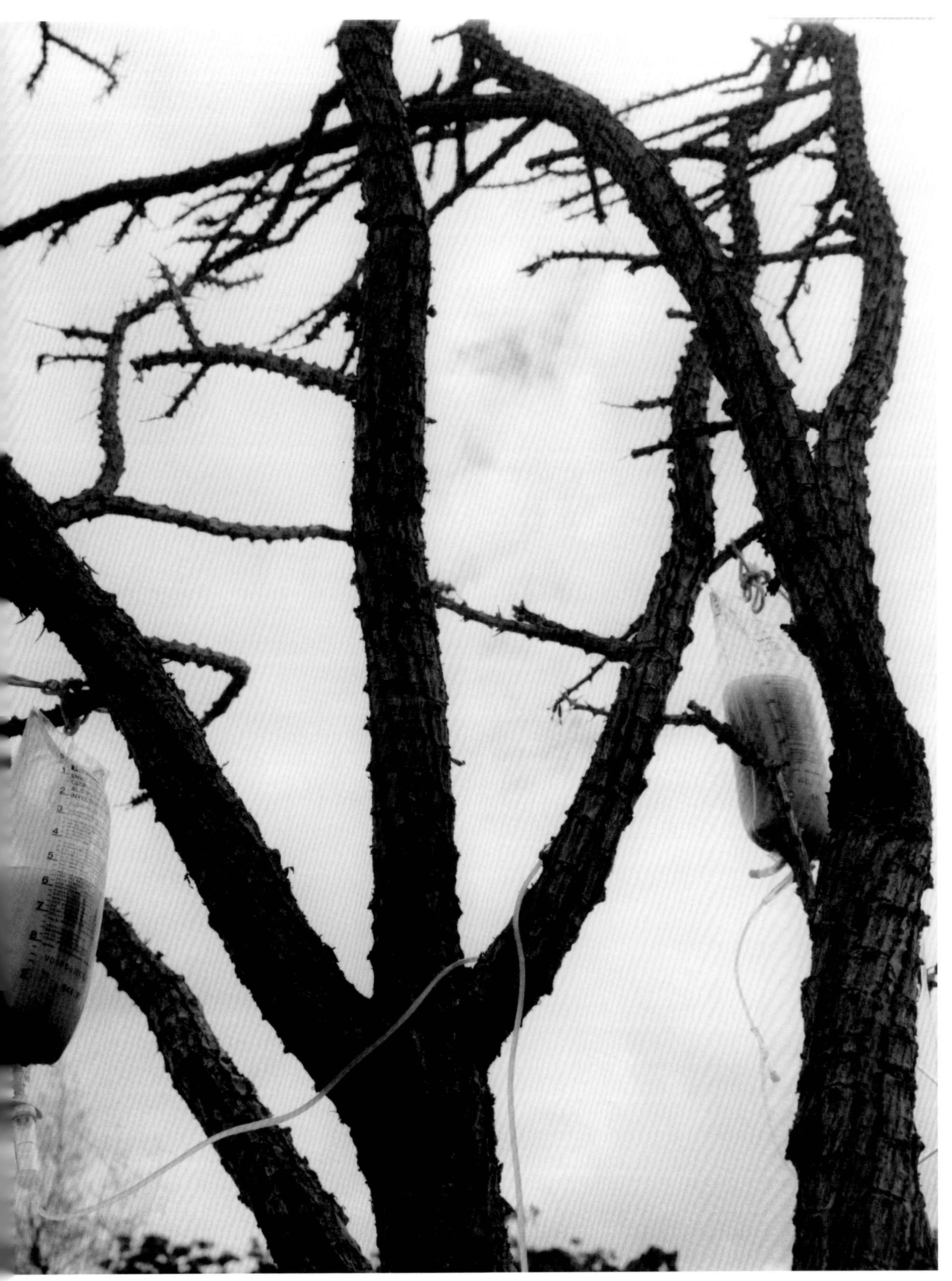

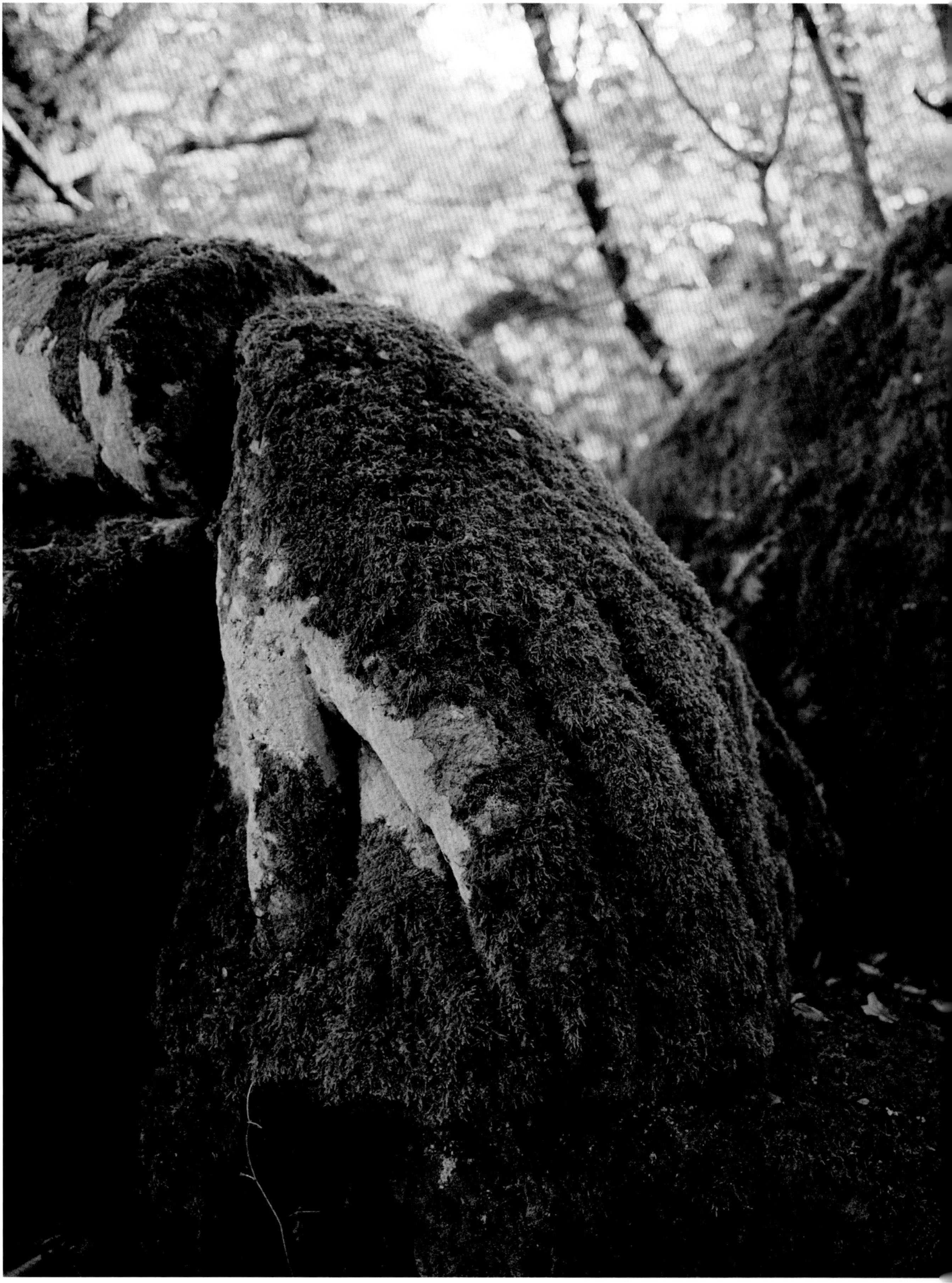

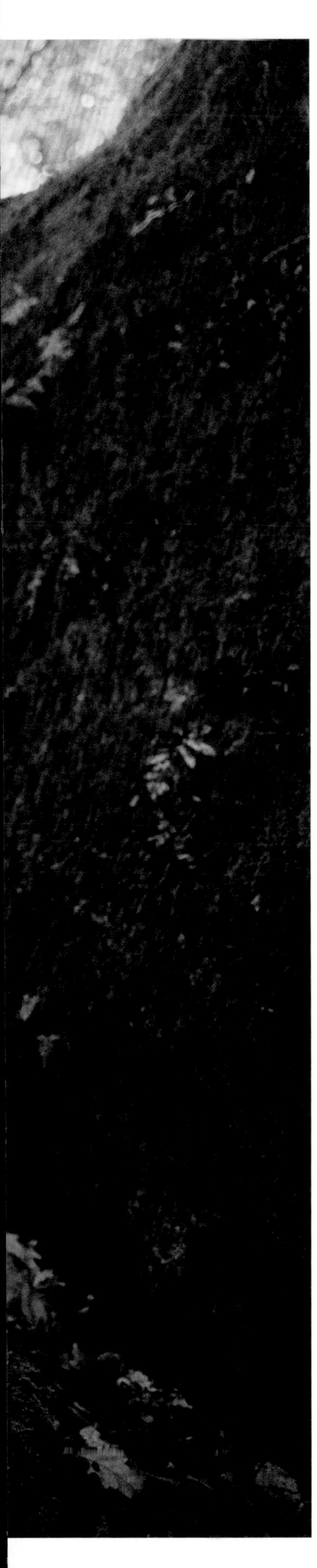

Graciela Iturbide
Untitled, Bomarzo, Italy, 2001

Origins

My images have become more silent and reflective with time. My gaze has shifted to the open sky, to landscape, to nature. In recent years, I have felt myself drawn to what's elemental: rocks, water, air, clouds, dust. My quest for primal forces is just beginning, and I do not know where it will lead. I was reading Roger Caillois and it dawned on me that my interest in stones lies in the fact that they are witnesses to a remote, prehuman past. They go back to the origin of everything we know, to the origin of life, to the Big Bang. The celestial fire created rock as it cooled.

I collect stones I find especially beautiful—one with white veins running through it has been with me for thirty years, and I have not tired of looking at it. I have meteorites from Bolivia, and when I look at them, I am still amazed that they are fragments of stars. I am struck by the uses that different civilizations have made of stones: religious, architectural, artistic, scientific, industrial. Our entire history is inscribed in stone. They help us to answer the question of where we come from.

When I photograph stones, as I have done in many places around the world, I try to let them be seen in their built or natural environments with all their richness of form and texture intact, and without any other presence to distract from contemplating them.

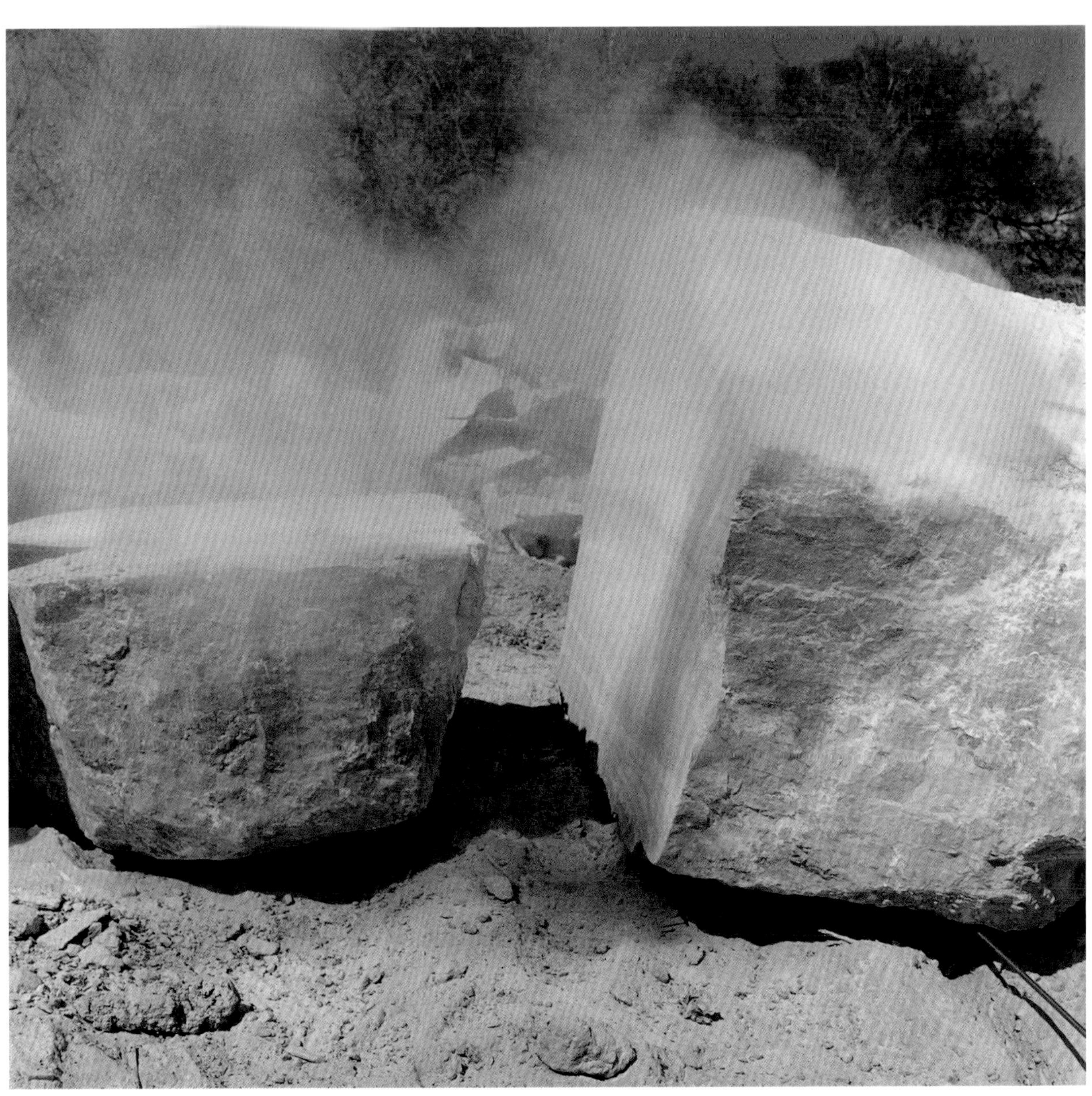

Graciela Iturbide
Untitled, Tecali de Herrera,
Puebla, Mexico, 2011

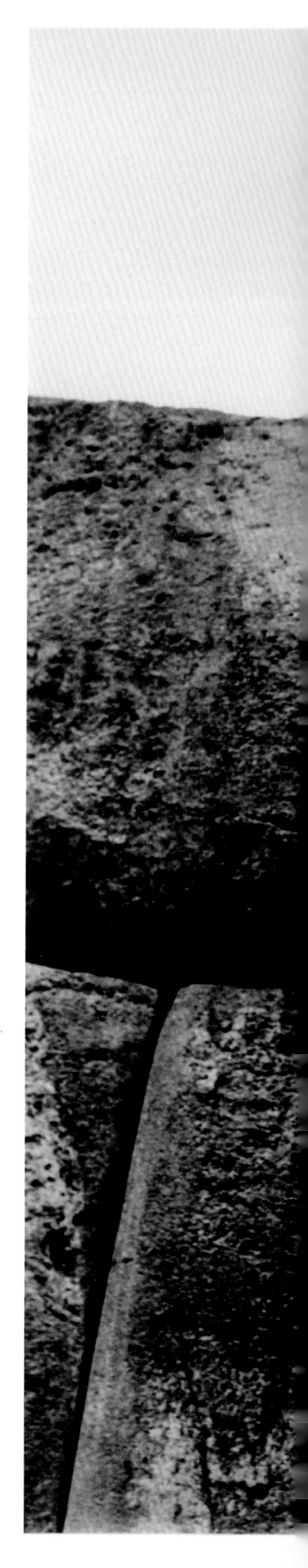

Graciela Iturbide
Untitled, Cusco, Peru, 2013

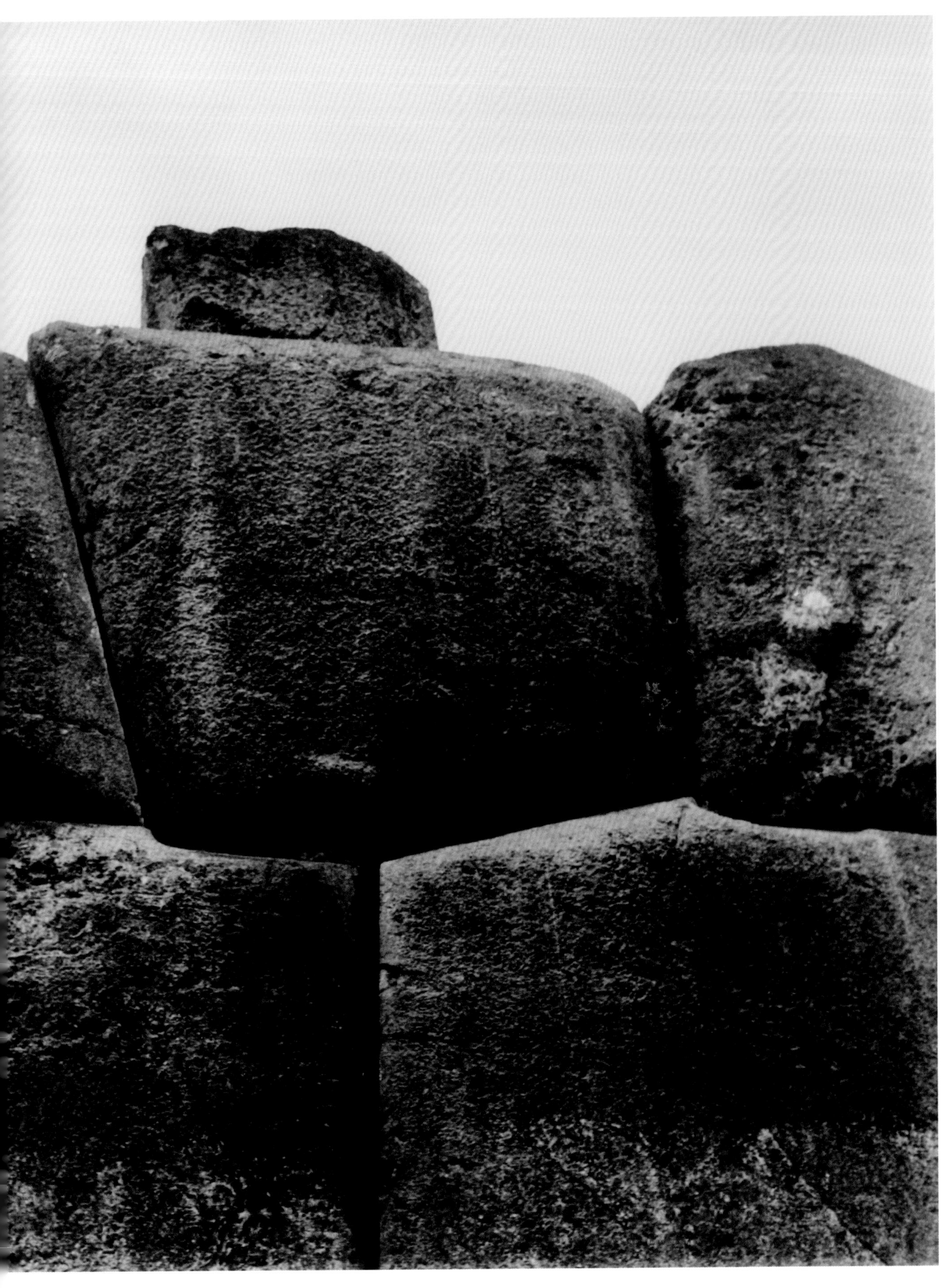

I only took two photographs of this stone resting at the entrance to the botanical gardens in Oaxaca. Just after taking the photo, I asked someone the time, so I could be sure to make an appointment; it was 4:30. Later that evening, Francisco Toledo informed me that my mother had passed away. He offered to stay with me, but I preferred to be alone. In speaking with my brothers and sisters, I realized that her death took place at the same time I took the photograph. My mother, Graciela Guerra, died at age eighty-one. The stone became a sort of shroud, a gravestone to me.

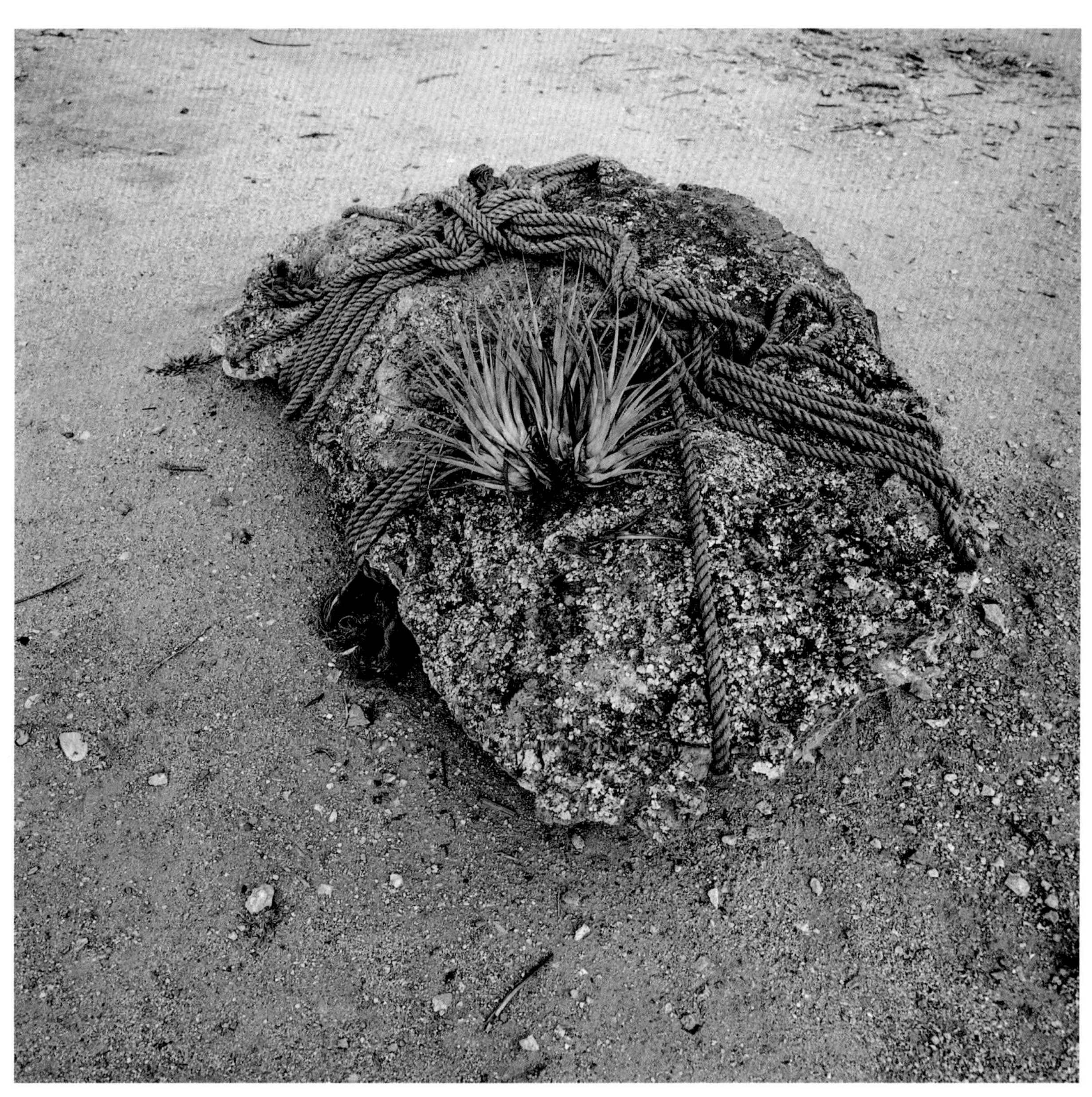

Graciela Iturbide
Jardín Botánico (Botanical Garden),
Oaxaca, Mexico, 2005

The Spark

I don't know whether my photography serves a purpose—it does not seek to convey a message. The pleasure of making images, of sustaining a vision of the world with them, of sharing them, enriches my life and helps me to go on living.

People often describe my images as *magical*, but I much prefer the term *poetic*, which is more difficult to achieve and more genuine. Photography should be poetic; images succeed when they transform reality thanks to a combination of sensibility and skill. Henri Cartier-Bresson said it this way: "Poetry is the essence of everything, and it's through deep contact with reality and living fully that you reach poetry. Very often I see photographers cultivating the strangeness or awkwardness of a scene, thinking it is poetry. No. Poetry is two elements which are suddenly in conflict—a spark between two elements. But it's given very seldom, and you can't look for it. It's like if you look for inspiration. No, it just comes by enriching yourself and living."

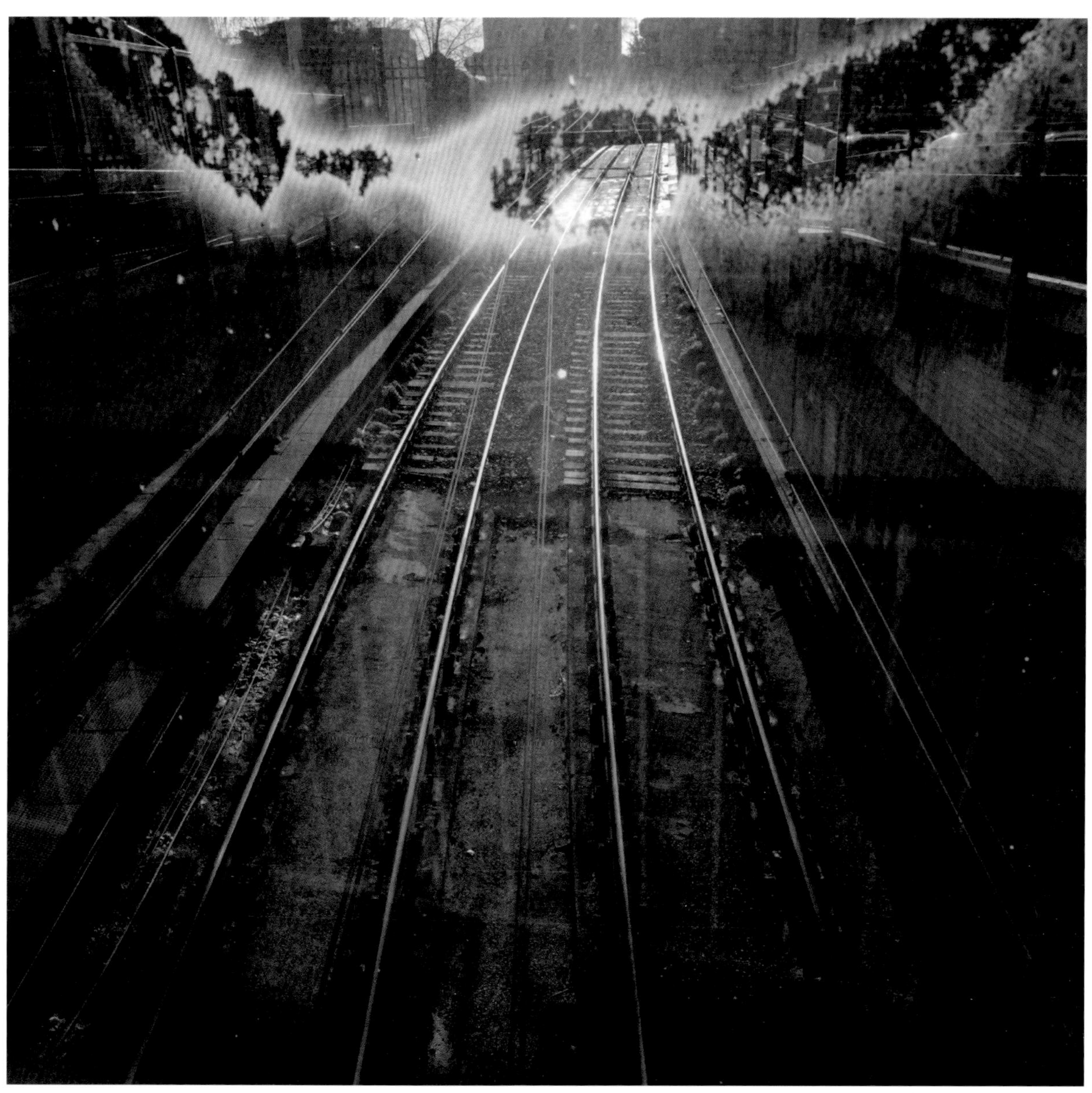

Graciela Iturbide
Cerca de Campos de Fiori
(Near Campo de' Fiori),
Rome, Italy, 2007

Further Reading

Books by Graciela Iturbide

Avándaro, text by Luis Carrión. Mexico City: Editorial Diógenes, 1971.

Los que viven en la arena (Those who live in the sand), text by Luis Barjau. Mexico City: INI-Fonapas, 1981.

Sueños de papel (Paper dreams), text by Verónica Volkow. Mexico City: Fondo de Cultura Económica, 1985.

Juchitán de las Mujeres (Women of Juchitán), text by Elena Poniatowska. Mexico City: Ediciones Toledo, 1989.

En el nombre del padre (In the name of the father), text by Osvaldo Sánchez. Mexico City: Ediciones Toledo, 1993.

Fiesta und Ritual: Graciela Iturbide's Mexiko (Festival and Ritual: Graciela Iturbide's Mexico), texts by Erika Billeter and Verónica Volkow. Salenstein, Switzerland: Benteli, 1994.

Images of the Spirit, texts by Alfredo López Austin and Roberto Tejada. New York: Aperture, 1996.

La forma y la memoria (form and memory), text by Carlos Monsiváis. Mexico: Museo de Arte Contemporáneo de Monterrey, 1996.

Graciela Iturbide, text by Cuauhtémoc Medina. London: Phaidon, 2001.

Pájaros (Birds), texts by José Luis Rivas and Bruce Wagner. Santa Fe, New Mexico: Twin Palms Publishers, 2002.

Graciela Iturbide habla con Fabienne Bradu (Graciela Iturbide in conversation with Fabienne Bradu). Madrid: La Fábrica; Fundación Telefónica, 2003.

Naturata, text by Fabio Morábito. Mexico City: Galería López Quiroga; Paris: Toluca Editions, 2004.

Graciela Iturbide, text by Marta Gili. Madrid: TF Editores, 2005.

Eyes to Fly With: Portraits, Self-Portraits, and Other Photographs, texts by Fabienne Bradu and Alejandro Castellanos. Austin: University of Texas Press, 2006.

Graciela Iturbide: Juchitán, text by Judith Keller. Los Angeles: J. Paul Getty Museum, 2007.

El baño de Frida Kahlo (Frida Kahlo's bathroom), text by Mario Bellatin. Mexico City: Editorial RM, 2009.

Graciela Iturbide, edited by Robert Delpire and Michel Frizot. Arles, France: Actes Sud; Paris: Photo Poche, 2011.

Graciela Iturbide: No hay nadie (There is no one), text by Óscar Pujol. Madrid: La Fábrica, 2011.

México-Roma. Mexico City: Editorial RM, 2011.

Graciela Iturbide, text by Lucía Alonso. Mexico City: Editorial RM; Puebla, Mexico: Museo Amparo, 2012.

Mi ojo (My eye). Mexico City: Editorial RM, 2016.

Des oiseaux (On birds), text by Guilhem Lesaffre. Paris: Èditions Xavier Barral, 2019.

Graciela Iturbide: cuando habla la luz (when the light speaks), text by Juan Rafael Coronel Rivera. Mexico City: Fomento Cultural Banamex, 2019.

Graciela Iturbide's Mexico, texts by Kristen Gresh and Guillermo Sheridan. Boston: Museum of Fine Arts, 2019.

Piedras (Stones). Mexico City: Editorial RM, 2019.

Heliotropo 37, texts by Fabienne Bradu and Eduardo Halfon. Paris: Fondation Cartier pour l'art contemporain, 2022.

THE PHOTOGRAPHY WORKSHOP SERIES

Graciela Iturbide

on Dreams, Symbols, and Imagination

Photographs and texts by Graciela Iturbide
Introduction by Alfonso Morales Carrillo
Edited by Alfonso Morales Carrillo and Mauricio Maillé

First edition, 2022
Printed in China
10 9 8 7 6 5 4 3 2 1

Front cover (clockwise from top left): *Magnolia con espejo* (Magnolia with mirror), Juchitán, Oaxaca, Mexico, 1986; *Cayó del cielo* (Fallen from heaven), Chalma, Mexico, 1984; Untitled, Jaipur, India, 1999; *Pájaros* (Birds), Dolores Hidalgo, Guanajuato, Mexico, 1978; *¿Ojos para volar?* (Eyes to fly with?), Coyoacán, Mexico City, 1991
Back cover (from top): Untitled, Sonoran Desert, Mexico, 1979; *Procesión* (Procession), Chalma, Mexico, 1984; *El viaje* (The voyage), Tlaxcala, Mexico, 1995

Editor: Denise Wolff
Assistant Editor: Lanah Swindle
Designer: Ann Griffin, Zürich
Production Director: Minjee Cho
Production Manager: Andrea Chlad
Production Consultant: Thomas Bollier
Copy Editor: Alexa Dilworth
Senior Text Editor: Susan Ciccotti
Proofreader: Elena Goukassian
Work Scholars: Isabella Convertino, Djuna Schamus

The staff of the Aperture book program includes:
Sarah Meister, Executive Director; Lesley A. Martin, Creative Director; Taia Kwinter, Publishing Manager; Emily Patten, Publishing Associate; Michael Famighetti, Editor, *Aperture* magazine; Brendan Embser, Senior Managing Editor, *Aperture* magazine; Karina Eckmeier, Designer; Kellie McLaughlin, Chief Sales and Marketing Officer; Richard Gregg, Sales Director, Books; Giada De Agostinis, Publicist

Translated from Spanish by Gregory Dechant

The Photography Workshop Series is made possible, in part, with generous support from S. B. Cooper and Rebecca Besson and the Besson/Cooper Fund.

Aperture's programs are made possible, in part, by the New York State Council on the Arts with the support of the Office of the Governor and the New York State Legislature.

Library of Congress Control Number: 2022900175
ISBN 978-1-59711-370-0

To order Aperture books, or inquire about gift or group orders, contact:
+1 212.946.7154
orders@aperture.org

For information about Aperture trade distribution worldwide, visit:
aperture.org/distribution

The seeds of many of the texts here began as interviews, principally by Mauricio Maillé and Alfonso Morales Carrillo for this publication, also by Fabienne Bradu—from *Eyes to Fly With* (2006) and *Conversaciones con fotógrafos: Graciela Iturbide habla con Fabienne Bradu* (2003)— as well as Christian Caujolle, Clément Chéroux, Diego Rabasa, Julio Rangel, and Ramón Reverté.

aperture

548 West 28th Street, 4th Floor
New York, NY 10001
aperture.org

Aperture, a not-for-profit foundation, connects the photo community and its audiences with the most inspiring work, the sharpest ideas, and with each other—in print, in person, and online.